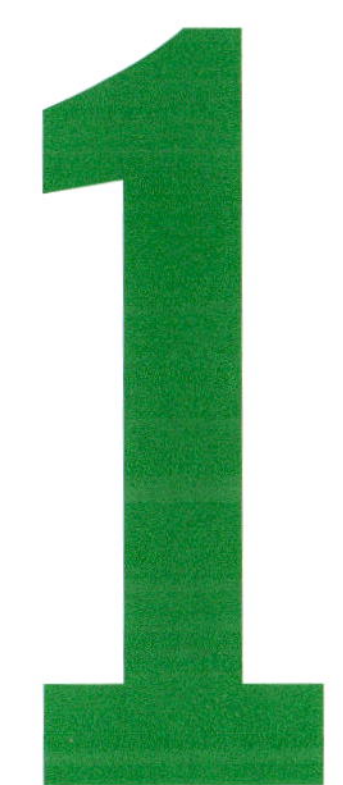

SUCCESS IN SOCCER

Basic Training

Techniques and Tactics for Developing the Serious Player (Ages 6-14)

by Gero Bisanz and Norbert Vieth

Published by the German Soccer Association (DFB) in conjunction with the DFB´s training staff: Berti Vogts, Rainer Bonhof, Hannes Löhr, Erich Rutemöller, Klaus Sammer, Bernd Stöber, Christina Theune-Meyer

Publishing House: Philippka-Verlag, P.B. 6540, D-48034 Münster

Published as volume 1 of the series of textbooks „Success in Soccer"

Editor: German Soccer Association (DFB)

DFB-coordinator: Frank Ludolph

Editing of the series: Gero Bisanz, Director of Coaching of the German Soccer Association (DFB)

Final editing: Dietrich Späte

Production manager: Werner Böwing

Layout and design: Siegmar Förster, Thorsten Krybus (Cover)

Translations: Anne Lendermann, Manni Klar

Cover photo and photo series: Ralph Woschny

Photos: Gero Breloer (page 7), Erich Baumann (page 9), Ralph Woschny (pages 25, 28, 61, 66, 68), Volker Minkus (page 26), Horst Müller (page 51, 59)

Printing: Holterdorf, Oelde/Germany

Contents

Some two years ago, the German Soccer Association laid the foundations for a new series of textbooks by publishing this volume. Quite deliberately we chose to target the first volume in the series at supervisors and coaches of junior players. For when youngsters aged between 6 and 14 years of age are taught the fundamentals of soccer in an educationally, methodologically and didactically sound way, they will be well on the way to future success.
The decisive factor here is that the people who teach the youngsters these first basic skills – i.e. coaches and supervisors, many of whom have no formal soccer training themselves – should be able to fall back on optimal coaching material.
The feedback on volume 1 of the DFB's new series of textbooks was so positive that the German Soccer Association was delighted to follow up on the proposal to produce the book in English as well, thereby extending its readership to a virtually limitless number. From our everyday experience in our organization's Frankfurt headquarters we know just how great the worldwide demand for simple, readily understandable teaching material for the trainers of our youngest soccer players really is.
Every day, we at the DFB, like UEFA and FIFA, receive requests for teaching material of this kind.
The German Soccer Association looks forward to producing a publication in the form of the book *Basic Training* with which it can meet the requirements of development aid in the sports sector and which supplements the new English-language magazine *Success in Soccer* due for publication in early 1998.

Egidius Braun

Egidius Braun, President of the German Soccer Association

Successes are seldom a matter of chance. Far more often they are the result of a long, hard slog.

The German Soccer Association (DFB) adopted this attitude a long time ago in its promotion of youth soccer and has always taken care to ensure that players of all ages receive top-notch supervision, both in theoretical and practical aspects of the game.

In "Basic Training", volume 1 of the new textbook series "Success in Soccer", the DFB's training staff continues this work in a far-sighted, unselfish manner.

Unselfish in that the DFB is also letting its teaching material be translated into English and French, thereby making its vast store of soccer knowledge available to a group of coaches right around the world.

FIFA welcomes this initiative launched by one of its largest and most successful associations and wishes to thank the authors and the DFB for their efforts designed to benefit the sport of soccer.

Joseph S. Blatter, General Secretary of FIFA

Where there is a ball, there will be players chasing it: Soccer unites people, and in European soccer, frontiers have been non-existent for a long time now. While many stars playing for top European clubs may be „foreigners", they are hugely popular with the local crowds, quite irrespective of their nationality.

Likewise, the coaching and development areas are growing ever closer together. Great strides have already been made towards the creation of a UEFA Coaching diploma system.

Nevertheless, it is youth soccer and the promotion of young talent where a united European approach becomes increasingly important. After all, these young players are Europe's footballing capital of the future. UEFA's various youth competitions are an important stepping stone as they provide the stars of the future with an early opportunity to prove themselves on the international scene.

By then, any top youth player worth his salt should be fully conversant with the essentials of the game. In the final analysis, it will always be the grassroots clubs which set the stage for attractive and successful soccer at top level. Any coach working there is teacher, psychologist and protector all rolled into one. On and off the pitch, these coaches greatly influence their pupils' development as human beings and footballers alike.

Therefore, the quality of European soccer tomorrow is very much a function of the quality of teaching and promoting talent today.

UEFA expressly welcomes the efforts made by the German Soccer Association (DFB) to provide all grassroots clubs with new and up-to-date technical literature. I am confident the DFB's initiative will provide other soccer nations with some valuable teaching materials for inclusion in their development programmes.

Andy Roxburgh, Director of the Technical Department of UEFA

Now you, too, can help shape the future of our soccer!

Gero Bisanz
Director of Coaching

Norbert Vieth
Editor of the DFB´s journal for coaches „fußballtraining“

Performance levels in international soccer are continuing to develop apace. In other words, the demands made on today´s top soccer players are already huge but tomorrow´s players will have to display even greater „technical playing perfection“. Such ideal players do not simply emerge as if by magic – they can only be produced by encouraging and promoting promising talent in a performance-oriented manner.

The present situation regarding youth soccer at club level is certainly not an easy one. On the other hand, though, there are many positive trends which allow us to look to the future with optimism:

The level of enthusiasm for soccer shown by the very young continues to be enormous. Never before have there been so many youth teams (6-8 year olds) at club level as there are today.

So the potential is there for attractive and successful soccer in the future. All that has to be done is to thoroughly exhaust this pool of talent on the basis of a modern, attractive and efficient concept for up-and-coming young players.

Coaches are the driving force behind encouraging and promoting talent to guarantee future success. In the first two books in this new DFB series, we want to provide this key target group with a practical guide for working with up-and-coming young players in a fun, deliberately structured, modern manner that is tailored to specific relevant age groups.

Besides numerous tips for planning and organizing training as well as for looking after youngsters, the book focuses mainly on the many possible variations of soccer games played in small teams when training our young players.

All that remains is for us to wish you a great deal of pleasure and every success!

Gero Bisanz Norbert Vieth

CHAPTER 1

Basic knowledge

BUILDING BLOCKS OF TRAINING WHEN WORKING WITH YOUNG PLAYERS

Soccer crazy

On any Saturday afternoon in Germany, virtually everywhere throughout the country, children and youngsters are out on the sports fields running after that familiar leather ball, fighting for it with great enthusiasm and maximum effort.

At the same time, tens of thousands of spectators stream into the soccer stadiums of the teams in the German Bundesliga. Germany's premier division is booming as never before. Those who cannot see "their" Bundesliga team perform live feverishly listen to the match commentary on the radio. This nationwide enthusiasm proves that soccer is without doubt the number one sport in Germany. Millions of soccer fans identify with the game. The German Football Association, for example, has over 6 million club members. There are around 150,000 teams battling for goals and points in all the various divisions and age categories.

The national team is a wonderful advertisement for German soccer thanks to its amazing achievement of winning World Cups and European Championships.

The reasons for the 'phenomenon' of soccer are many and varied. The 'soccer bug' has many causes.

Absolutely fundamental is the simplicity of the very idea of the game, which can be briefly summarized as "to score goals and prevent the opposing team from scoring any". The rules are correspondingly simple and can therefore be grasped rapidly. Anyone can play soccer. All that is needed is 'something round' – it does not even have to be a proper ball – and a marked-out goal. Even individuals with little talent for sport can organize and enjoy a 'proper' game of soccer using the simplest of resources.

Even if the action on the pitch has a somewhat 'ungainly' appearance when beginners or less experienced soccer players, everybody has a chance in the game of soccer. The fascination exercised by the game is apparent right from the very beginning.

Soccer a 'self-starter'?

Does this make soccer a 'self-starter' amongst young players, then? Much suggests that this is the case. However, forward-looking work in youth soccer must take on new areas of responsibility and tackle the problem areas head on. Having said this, everyone involved in and committed to youth soccer can count on at least one very valuable ally, namely the game of soccer itself! The important thing is to keep the fascination of the game alive in all the age groups.

The four building blocks of a modern youth coaching concept set out here can provide all coaches of youngsters with valuable tips, guidance and hints.

1 The fun element

How can we make the game attractive and enjoyable for youngsters?

2 Looking to the future

What must the soccer player of tomorrow learn today?

3 Taking age into account

What should be learned when?

4 Remaining up-to-date

What do young players expect from a club?

1 The fun element

How can we make the game attractive and enjoyable for youngsters?

First contacts with a soccer ball – in the past and now

Today as much as at any time in the past, children and young people are still attracted to playing with that familiar round leather ball. Young players are gripped by the sheer enjoyment of playing the game and this lures them to places where they can play soccer. In the past, their initial soccer experience was gained kicking a ball around on the streets, in back gardens, fields, or the local park. Wherever there was a bit of room to play, soccer-crazy kids would congregate. And time and time again they showed a great deal of imagination in 'inventing' new rules to tailor the game to the situation at hand.

Big and smaller kids used to play together for hours on end, displaying tremendous enthusiasm. Playing, battling, laughing (and sometimes also arguing) – that sums up 'street soccer', the day-to-day 'training' of young players in the good old days. Children and youngsters created their own world of play in which they found their place and felt happy.

In these kids' games played on the street, they learnt what they needed later for 'grown-up soccer'.

So how are the first serious contacts with that round leather ball made nowadays?

Today children play a lot less soccer in their spare time. Even the areas made available for informal kick-arounds often remain unused. Children's soccer has moved into the organized club environment. Never have there been so many youth soccer teams (6-8 year olds) at club level as there are today. So access to the sport of soccer is quite different these days. And yet the reasons for this trend have precious little to do with the game of soccer itself, the main reason being that a childhood today is substantially different from what it used to be, especially in such important areas of life as the family, friends and school. And these changes are taking place at an ever more furious pace. In the course of these developments, playing soccer has acquired quite a different level of importance today.

For this reason, the wish to revive 'street soccer' in all its former glory is illusory.

In spite of – or maybe precisely because of – these developments, children today have all the more right to experience and enjoy playing. And if children's chief contact with the favourite game of soccer now occurs mainly in clubs, these organizations must give children the chance to experience the carefree enjoyment of street soccer as it used to be!

In the past, playing soccer with some friends was far more important to youngsters. This was the level at which up-and-coming players acquired the technique required for 'grown-up soccer' played at club level later.

Unfortunately, however, the reality of youth soccer is often quite different:

■ During a match, junior players are inundated from all sides by cheers and shouts of encouragement, but also by reproaches and threats. The latter generate fear, which suppresses the youngsters' creativity and adventurousness. Young club players have practically no chance any more of enjoying a carefree, informal game of soccer. Children in the younger age groups adapt their own game, either consciously or unconsciously, to the clamour of demands shouted by their coaches, supervisors or parents. In this way, adults destroy children's enjoyment of the game, thus hindering the development of individual ideas as well as children's independence and self-confidence to develop their own way of playing.

N.B.

How to make soccer enjoyable at club level:

● **Children want to play soccer free of all duress:**
- **just for themselves according to their own rules,**
- **without being greatly influenced by the trainer,**
- **without being told what to do by their parents,**
- **in line with their own wishes,**
- **at a level matching their own capabilities,**
- **in small groups.**

These are the elements which create maximum enjoyment and sow the seed for a life-long enthusiasm for soccer. Only in this way will playing soccer be a pleasurable experience for children.

● **The children's game must not be allowed to become like the adults' game.**

● **There is no place in children's soccer for adults telling them what to do or imposing overly narrow rules or constraints on them!**

● **Coaches must deliberately hold back when working with the very young. Although they must display enthusiasm and show their readiness to help, their main duty is to encourage and organize informal and carefree games of soccer for the youngest junior players. They will then have fulfilled their main task!**

This type of soccer is certainly not a game for children!

■ A lot of valuable playing experience is also hindered by inappropriately organized practices. All too often practice, especially in the younger age groups, is dominated by outdated exercises which disrupt the players' motivation because they only teach individual elements of technique taken from the broad spectrum of the game. But fine-tuning individual elements of technique makes no sense whatsoever if the children concerned have not yet been able to develop adequate playing skills and their actual enjoyment is spoiled by negative playing experiences.

From all of the above we can derive a fundamental guideline for organizing youth coaching:

Children must initially learn to experience and love soccer as a carefree **game**. Only then will they develop a fascination for soccer and the foundations will be laid for their life-long love of the game.

The main emphasis of soccer training for children should therefore be focused on the many different possibilities offered by games of soccer played in small groups. The 'street soccer' of the past needs a new 'home' in the clubs of today.

2 Looking to the future

What must the soccer players of tomorrow learn today?

Top-class performance over the long term

The wishes and needs of children interested in soccer must always serve as the basis for organizing youth training.

Primarily, they want to **play** soccer with other kids. Consequently, the prime task facing anyone training juniors is to encourage the children's spontaneity and enjoyment of soccer by providing a host of simple, attractive experiences in the form of games played in small groups. This fundamentally playful outlook must go on to remain the guiding principle throughout the entire youth training phase!

On the other hand, soccer training must amount to something more than just letting kids play. After all, children who join a soccer club want to learn to play soccer properly.

Indeed, the objective of any performance-oriented nurturing of young talent is to develop adult soccer players boasting the highest possible level of ability.

But when all is said and done a high – or the highest – level of performance can only be achieved if systematic training takes place -

ight from the start of youth coaching.

Only a long-term, continuous enhancement of players' performance can constitute a basis for a successful and attractive game all the way up to top-class soccer.

The demands of soccer as a team game

Let us begin by taking a detailed look at the individual elements of the team game of soccer, which must at the same time constitute the individual aspects of all youth training programs. All the other complex demands of the sport are derived from the basic aim of the game, which we have already described simply as scoring and preventing goals.

■ Only those players truly mastering the many varied *technical skills* required in the game will be able to reach this objective.

■ At the same time, playing soccer makes high and varied *demands on players' fitness*. For instance, even the best technicians have to win one-against-one races for the ball (speed) and be able to play precision passes in the dying minutes of a game (stamina).

Nowadays, the so-called *basic coordination required* to play the game well is considered much more important than it was in the past. What is meant by this is children's all-round mobility and ball skill, which initially does not just involve skills that are specific to soccer, but extends far beyond them. Basic coordination is essential if players are to prove capable of learning complicated soccer techniques more quickly and to a higher degree of perfection.
Only on this solid basis can soccer players subsequently acquire a wide range of playing skills.

■ But even optimal basic ability in an individual player and the individual achievements this makes possible will ultimately not bear fruit unless they can be embedded into *team play*.
Youth players must therefore learn how to fit into a group (and not only on the pitch!). They must combine with their team-mates, help each other and share the complex tasks of the game.

■ After all, soccer is always a game played against another team. An individual player's actions in the game – whether acting or reacting – must also always be geared to the behaviour of the players on the opposing teams. This constant working with each other and against each other results in complex *tactical demands* being made on individual players, a group of players or the entire team.

■ Soccer must always be played in accordance with mandatory rules. Junior players must be told what the sense and purpose of such rules is. They must then learn them and comply with them when playing competitive matches.

Demands of tomorrow's soccer

The team game of soccer makes many different kinds of demands on individual players and these demands help us to pinpoint important objectives in any youth training program.

These demands have to be met by young players if they want to be successful at playing soccer nowadays. However, the game is constantly developing, which means that the demands made on top players are both increasing and constantly evolving.

A concept for juniors geared towards training the top players of tomorrow by encouraging and promoting promising talent in a performance-oriented manner must also – indeed, in particular – take account of forward-looking trends.

So what will be the special characteristics of attractive and successful soccer of *tomorrow*?

THE GAME TOMORROW	THE PLAYERS OF TOMORROW
BASIC TRENDS	
■ Teams of the future must gear their own way of playing to particular *guiding principles*: – A basic attack-oriented attitude, i.e. a basically offensive outlook – Effective and, at the same time, attractive style of play – A fundamentally fair attitude ■ Fast *pace of the game*: fast action throughout the 90 minutes (and extra time) and in all positions. ■ High degree of *tactical flexibility* on the part of the team and individual players, involving the swift adaptation of play to the relevant game situation.	■ Technical perfection: – Well-honed ball skills – "Creativity on the ball" – Mastering of all basic techniques (dribbling, passing/shooting techniques, ball control, heading, etc.) even in games played at full tilt, in the tightest spaces and when under pressure ■ High level of individual ability as the basis for a broad range of group and team-tactical elements. ■ High level of fitness (speed, stamina, coordination).
ELEMENTS OF DEFENSE	
■ Ball-oriented, active defending: – Situation-specific shifting of play according to the run of the ball with a view to putting the opponents under pressure – Objective: winning possession of the ball quickly and initiating own attacks, e.g. by intercepting passes. Merely 'breaking up' the opposition's attacks is not sufficient. ■ Safe build-up of play from the back. ■ Fouls must not be allowed to become a tactical weapon!	■ Optimum defense reaction in all positions: – Rapid appreciation of changing possibilities for attacking – Basic principles: high level of individual tactical ability, speed, skilfulness, toughness and willpower ■ Technically proficient defenders capable of initiating creative build-up play from the back. ■ No unnecessary fouls!
ELEMENTS OF ATTACK	
■ Well thought-out, creative solo moves as the basis for collective attacks. ■ Fast, flexible combination play involving long and short passes – no 'knocking the ball about at high speed'. ■ Determined, adventurous, flexible and technically perfect finishing, even when under maximum pressure from the opposition.	■ Technically perfect attackers playing with finesse and determination, but who are also assertive and adventurous: – Large repertoire of moves for getting past a player on the opposing team (e.g. feints, body swerves, sending players the wrong way, etc.) – Good, safe combination play – Definitely goal-hungry! ■ Offensive qualities in *all* playing positions

3 Taking age into account

What should be learned when?

From a beginner to be a top soccer player

The road from enthusiastic beginner to widely acclaimed top soccer player is, as everyone knows, a long one.
So what is the best way of guaranteeing the specific, systematic practice process needed to make the transformation?

1st step:
Establishing a set of individual practice objectives

To recap: the aim of youth coaching is to coach youngsters to play forward-looking, attractive and successful soccer. This makes complex demands on players in the areas of their technique, tactics, fitness and mental attitude.
For children's and youth coaching, this initially grossly excessive set of requirements associated with adult soccer has to be broken down into smaller mini-objectives which build on each other systematically and can gradually be geared towards the more ambitious objective within the context of a long-term training process.
In practice this means dividing up the practice program into clearly defined phases which are, initially, relatively independent of the players' age.
For example: youngsters cannot be trained to play down the wings until the basic technical and tactical prerequisites, e.g. dribbling skill, the ability to kick the ball with the instep and head the ball, have been worked on.
If individual stages are left out when working on these mini-objectives, gaps will inevitably be left which will be difficult to fill later in the training process. Thorough, stable development therefore requires time, consistency and patience!

2nd step:
Adapting the mini-objectives of coaching to the developmental phases of young players

The 'typical' course of physical and mental development from childhood to adulthood can be divided up into individual phases. This results in so-called 'development stage' models which can serve to guide coaches in their work on training and supervising youth players.
On the other hand, however, coaches must not ignore the special individual qualities of each youth player.
The age groups and developmental characteristics of the individual stages described can, in all cases, only be taken as rough guides. The transition point from one stage to the next can vary.
Despite these restrictions, systematic youth practice must be based on a step by step model of this kind. The reason for this is that the various stages of soccer training have to be adapted to the specific situation applying during each developmental phase if the development-oriented enhancement of players' performance from their days as beginners to their careers as top players is to be guaranteed.
Within each age group, individual levels of development will influence the objectives, content, methods and demands of training.

The individual training phases

As a result, a concept comprising the following three phases is therefore appropriate for children's and youth training:

- Basic practice
- Intermediate practice
- Advanced practice

These phases of training must always include the main aspects of long-term performance build-up for which the young player has the best physical and mental qualifications based on his current level of development. The age group categories used by the DFB can easily be applied to these three phases of training.

BASIC TRAINING

This phase of training is for boys and girls between 7 and 10 years old. This is known as the "early school age" phase of development.

DEVELOPMENTAL CHARACTERISTICS

■ "First change of shape": the body's extremities (legs, arms) grow more quickly than the trunk and spinal column. At the same time, the organs of the cardio-vascular system increase in size.

■ This stage of development is more or less the same for both boys and girls, although individual children differ greatly in terms of their pattern of growth and physical development.

■ Typical characteristics for girls and boys:
- pronounced enjoyment of movement,
- highly competitive sprit,
- coordination-related difficulties,
- only poorly developed muscles,
- low powers of concentration,
- high level of sensitivity,
- strong, uncritical attitude towards adult 'idols'.

■ When they start school, children find themselves in a fundamentally new situation in life: The "playful atmosphere" of the parental home is replaced by school and the obligations that go with it. The child is now suddenly only one of many and has to fit into a larger group.

OBJECTIVES

■ To provide all-round athletic experience (basic coordination and fitness).

■ To teach the basic idea of the game, namely "scoring and preventing goals".

■ To learn the most important elements of technique (in their preliminary forms): dribbling, passing, shooting.

■ To teach the youngsters a (pre)tactical code of behaviour, i.e.:
- scoring goals as the result of teamwork and solo efforts,
- preventing goals and winning back the ball when the opposition is in possession,
- sticking to assigned areas and positions (though each child must play in all positions from goalkeeper to striker in training and games).

■ To encourage the sheer enjoyment of playing soccer.

■ To learn and experience group behaviour (helping/being helped, accepting others).

■ To make suggestions about additional sporting activities in the youngsters' free time.

■ To playfully learn the "minimum rules" (kick-off, throw-in, corner kick, free kick, penalty kick, goal kick).

CONTENT

■ Games and exercises for furthering ball skills:
- exercises involving rolling, bouncing and airborne balls,
- ball games played in small groups.

■ Additional games and exercises for furthering agility (running, hopping, jumping):
- games of tag/relays,
- obstacle courses,
- reflex exercises/balancing exercises/rhythmic exercises, occasionally using various sports equipment.

■ Motivating games and exercises for kids to learn the basic aspects of technique (dribbling, passing, shooting).

■ Free-and-easy games of soccer with small teams playing into goals:
- 2 against 2
- 3 against 3
- 4 against 4

■ Interesting tackling exercises involving a great deal of learning:
- 1 against 1 into one goal,
- 1 against 1 into two goals.

D JUNIORS (10-12 YEAR OLDS)

DEVELOPMENTAL CHARACTERISTICS

■ The special characteristic of D juniors is their balance between physical and, at the same time, mental development. This stage of their life is also referred to as the "golden age of learning" or "age of harmony".

■ Positive personal traits of D juniors include:
- self-confidence,
- interest,
- a willingness to learn,
- powers of observation,
- improved powers of concentration,
- enjoyment of movement and a readiness to perform competitively.

■ Their positive physical characteristics and qualities include:
- balanced physical appearance through a better proportioned body,
- greater coordination.

■ These qualities form an outstanding basis for their more specific learning of all the elements of the game of soccer.

OBJECTIVES

■ To systematically learn and consolidate technical skills:
- dribbling with the inside and outside of the foot, with the instep, as well as with many changes of speed and direction,
- playing with the inside and outside of the foot (especially safe passes),
- playing with the flat inside of the foot, as well as with the instep and outside of the foot (particularly for shooting and crossing the ball),
- controlling low, slightly lofted and high passes,
- heading the ball (standing still and on the run).

■ Variable application of basic techniques in different game situations (also when under pressure from an opposing player).

■ Using games to teach specific basic tactical principles used during play:
- running into space to lose a marker (by changing speed/feinting),
- passing combinations to safeguard possession of the ball and prepare to take a shot on goal.

■ Using games to consolidate basic playing fitness.

■ Imparting a positive attitude towards the game of soccer.

CONTENT

■ Individual motivating exercises for improving ball skills:
- different ways of changing direction,
- feints and other tricks for getting past opponents.

■ 1-on-1 training to secure possession of the ball or as a solo run to prepare for a shot at goal.

■ Games played in small groups with special emphasis on particular technical and tactical aspects:
- dribbling
- ball control,
- heading,
- shooting at goal, etc.

■ Boosting motivation by arranging competitions and games involving running to improve the children's agility.

■ Free-and-easy games with small teams shooting into two goals (e.g. in the form of a tournament).

■ Interesting circuit training with technical exercises alternating with games played in small groups.

INTERMEDIATE TRAINING

During this phase of training, girls and boys are at an age just before puberty. Differences in sexual development result in girls leaving this phase earlier (at the age of 11 or 12) than boys (12/13).

INTER-MEDIATE TRAINING

In this phase of training there are considerable differences between D (10-12 year olds) and C (12-14 year olds) juniors with regard to the objectives and aspects of training. The reason for this is that puberty normally begins in the C junior age group, which in-evitably has consequences for soccer training.

C JUNIORS (12-14 YEAR OLDS)

DEVELOPMENTAL CHARACTERISTICS

■ From around the age of 12 or 13, a change occurs in the children's stages of development, resulting in radical alterations in both their physical and mental condition:
- development of sexual maturity,
- accelerated upward growth.

■ The main consequences of these decisive physical and mental changes during puberty are, above all, the impairment of their powers of coordination and frequent mood swings.

■ Nevertheless, this stage of development does not necessarily have to be regarded as a "time of crisis" or "age of soft treatment".
At the same time, quite new physical and mental abilities (e.g. improved strength and a better understanding of the game) also emerge from the growth and maturity processes during puberty which can, with specific training tailored to the age in question, constitute a basis for further improvements in their performance.

OBJECTIVES

■ Adaptation of individual technical and tactical abilities to improved speed and strength (training and stabilization of "dynamic techniques").

■ Sporting and personal encouragement of individual youngsters depending on their respective stage of development.

■ Teaching more demanding tactical elements:
- use of space and positional play,
- running into space depending on the specific situation,
- group tactics in attack and defence,
- tasks associated with individual playing positions.

■ Motivating improvement and consolidation of basic principles of fitness:
- speed,
- basic stamina,
- all-round strengthening,
- agility!

■ Encouraging players' independent thinking and sense of responsibility.

■ Developing a consistent readiness to perform to enable specific and regular training.

CONTENT

■ Games and exercises with more demanding points of focus:
- various team-game possibilities,
- tasks associated with specific positions within the team.

■ Differentiated training for individual performance-related groups, e.g. in the form of:
- circuit training with various technical exercises,
- circuit training focusing on various aspects of fitness,
- circuit training with various exercises tailored to individual playing positions.

■ Assault course and stamina games/cross-country running (to occasionally supplement training).

■ Strengthening exercises (in pairs, with medicine balls, in the form of pulling and pushing contests).

■ Reflex and 'flying start' exercises, e.g. races for the ball with subsequent 1-on-1 confrontations until a goal is scored.

■ Agility programmes.

■ Informal games shooting into two goals (also in the form of a tournament).

Children's training

Children's training covers the ages from 6 to 14, i.e. the F, E, D and C juniors according to the DFB's age group categories. Children's training is split up into two phases:
The first section, **basic training**, is for 6 to 10-year-old youngsters (F and E juniors);
the second phase, **intermediate training**, covers the 10 to 12 age group (D juniors) as well as 12 to 14-year-olds (C juniors).

Youth training

Youth training covers 14 to 16-year-old boys and girls (B juniors) and 16 to 18-year-old boys (A juniors).
This phase of training is referred to as advanced training.
This phase of training is referred to as **advanced training**.

Children's and youth training is generally known internationally as "junior training".

Ideal course of training and "late starters"

Ideally then, junior training takes place between the ages of 6 and 16 for girls and until the age of 18 for boys.
All the key elements for successful and attractive soccer have to be taught gradually over this long period.
The best way of ensuring a sound, continuous build-up of performance is for children to start regular training at the early age of 6 to 8 years. If they do so, their age group, development phase and phase of training will then correspond all the way through their junior training.
If a youngster does not begin regular club training until somewhat later, the first phase of training no longer applies. As a rule, however, many boys have already acquired all-round experience of sport in general – and soccer in particular – outside the club, with the result that any deficiencies can be rectified relatively quickly through systematic training.
The situation is frequently different for girls. Often they have no previous experience of sport whatsoever, which means that, for them, the basic training content has to be included in the intermediate training program.
Coaches must show special understanding for junior players who have not undergone the first phase of training. They must carefully assess their playing and training performance and adapt the further learning process to rectify any deficiencies.

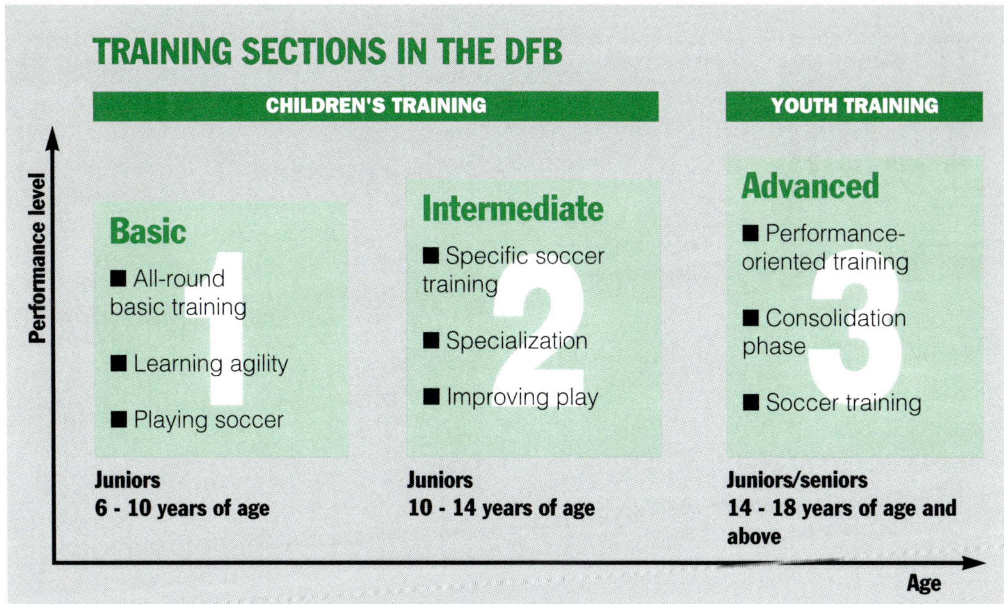

FROM 4-A-SIDE TO 11-A-SIDE

When fostering youth players, training and playing games must form an inseparable unit. For this reason, attractive and, in particular, age-specific training is not sufficient on its own. Official competitions must also be organized at every stage, tailored to the needs and abilities of the children or youngsters concerned. For this reason, the 11-a-side game has no place in the youngest age groups.

4-A-SIDE

Scheduled fixtures

F to D juniors (6-12 year olds)

■ In the younger age groups, 4-a-side tournaments must regularly supplement the official competitive season.

■ Fixed dates for these additional tournaments should be included in the playing schedule (e.g. the last weekend of each month).

■ These tournaments should be organized by a neighbouring club or the local district's soccer league.

In training

F to E juniors (6-10 year olds)

■ Of the two training units per week, one should consist entirely of an informal 4-a-side game shooting into two goals.

■ Trainers should only organize the game at the beginning. They should then observe the course of the game and offer assistance only where urgently required.

D to C juniors (10-12 year olds)

■ The 4-a-side game is varied with specific tasks and exercises in such a way that emphasis is placed on the training of particular technical and tactical elements.

Main aspects of competitive play

■ The 4-a-side game is the smallest possible form of the game in which all the essential technical and tactical elements of the 'adult' game occur and can be trained intensively:

– deliberate build-up play,

– creating and exploiting goal opportunities,

– setting up a solid defense.

■ This involves training focused on the basic principles of attractive, forward-looking play, namely variable team-play, creative solo runs, novel attacking ploys and an enthusiastic, solid defense geared towards winning back possession of the ball as quickly as possible.

■ Because of the small size of the team, all the players have to help each other at all times. The limited size of the pitch also enables junior players to follow everything that is going on.

■ Continuous involvement in the game, creativity and adventurousness must be demanded and encouraged in all playing situations.

7-A-SIDE

Scheduled fixtures

F to D juniors (6-12 year olds)

■ There is no place in the lowe age groups for the 11-a-side cc petitive game with large goals played on a full-size pitch!

■ 7-a-side games played on or half of a full-size pitch constitute the officially approved format fc this age group in league fixture

In training

C to A juniors (12-18 year olds)

■ Games involving smaller tear are also more effective when teaching higher age groups an are therefore a key element in t training program.

■ Tactical games played on lar pitches and in larger teams car course be used to supplement training program in order to trai essential team-tactical and pos tion-specific aspects.

ain aspects of ompetitive play

The 1-3-3 formation is ideal for
e 7-a-side game.

The guiding principle here is: the players must **always** be ven offensive and defensive sks.

There should be no sweeper aying behind the defence. This l encourage better, more re-onsible defensive play by all the ayers in 1-on-1 tackling situa-ns.

The players must be told to con-antly mark one player on the op-sing team and tackle with deter-nation.
epending on the game situation, wever, they should also move wards the ball with a view to win-ng back possession as quickly possible by having more ayers close to the ball. The ayers must be encouraged to lp each other (prompting, call-g, etc.).

Genuine attacking players must placed in all three forward posi-ns. This helps to train 'tricky' ngers and players with goalscor-g instincts.

11-A-SIDE

Scheduled fixtures

C to A juniors (12-18 year olds)

■ The "normal" 11-a-side game played on a full-size pitch may only be used for league games, etc. from the C junior category upwards!

■ However, there is nothing wrong with organizing a round of league games with 7-a-side teams on a smaller pitch in the older age groups if there are not enough players.

■ The top priority is to give all youngsters who are interested in soccer the chance to play and be motivated.

In training

B and A juniors (14-18 year olds)

■ Where the size of the training squad permits, 11-a-side training games can be slipped in every now and again in the two highest age groups with specific emphasis on team tactics.

■ However, having said that, games involving smaller teams incorporating set technical/tactical tasks and exercises are (as "parts of the big game") far more effective in the older age groups as well.

Main aspects of competitive play

■ The main basic formation appropriate for this age group is:

- 3 attacking forwards (outside right/centre forward/outside left)
- 3 midfield players
- 3 defenders (right back/left back/centre back)
- 1 sweeper (where possible level with or even **in front of** the row of defenders)
- 1 goalkeeper

■ In this way, the pitch will be evenly occupied and excessive, unnecessary running avoided. This will ensure greater emphasis being placed on technical and tactical skills than on fitness requirements.

■ Using a deliberate build-up, the ball can be played out of defense via midfield deep to the attacking forwards.

4 Remaining up-to-date

What do young players expect from a club?

Assessment of today's youth training

Children and youngsters today grow up in a different world to their parents. Attitudes towards active sport and playing soccer in a club environment have also changed because of this 'new' childhood and youth.

Inflexible youth training planned along the lines of: "We've always done it this way and that's the way things will stay!" is therefore doomed to failure sooner or later.

The excessive numbers of youngsters leaving clubs in the higher age groups give a very clear indication of the need to bring the training of youth players up to date. This raises the following fundamental questions:

- How can the sport of soccer be adapted to the interests of children and young people, i.e. how can it be presented in a more appropriate, modern and attractive manner tailored to the age groups concerned?
- How can regular fixtures be organized in a way that makes them more appealing to children and young people?
- How can children and young people be persuaded to play club soccer as opposed to the many other sports and leisure activities on offer?
- What needs do youth players have apart from playing soccer? Can clubs also offer something here?

This (self-critical) assessment of our own youth training does not mean that we suddenly have to offer a completely different range of programmes or draw up a totally different club outlook. That would also be asking far too much of the people working in the clubs. The fascination of playing soccer remains the key. So with this in mind, there is a need to carry out a critical review of the organization of fixtures and training activities as well as of the club environment itself. Are the soccer programmes provided by clubs really ideally geared to the interests and needs of today's different age groups? Where can improvements be made?
Getting these 'soccer fundamentals' right at youth level also makes it easier to plan and implement junior activities outside the area of sport.

Childhood yesterday and today

- Children first have to come to terms with the world in which they live.
- In this respect, 'movement' and 'play' represent extremely important opportunities for recognizing and exploring new space, establishing contacts, developing skills and gathering experience.
- The world of children is, above all, a world of play and recognition.
- This world of movement and play used to be 'the street', where children gathered to play familiar games together, thought up tricks to play on people and launched expeditions into 'uncharted territory'. Parents could only monitor all of this to a limited extent.
- This environment of movement and play has now gone. Today, children are taken off the street and placed solicitously and specifically in the care of soccer clubs, to take but one example.
- Consequently, clubs have replaced 'the street' as the main, more closely monitored, space for children to move about and play in.
- This means that children are having to content themselves with a world of soccer designed and supervised by adults. The freedom to amuse themselves has been replaced by organized training within a club environment.

Conclusion: Greater freedom must be created within the club for informal, carefree play, including soccer games. The coach must consciously take a back seat. His main job is to provide playing opportunities.

WHAT IS EXPECTED OF CLUBS

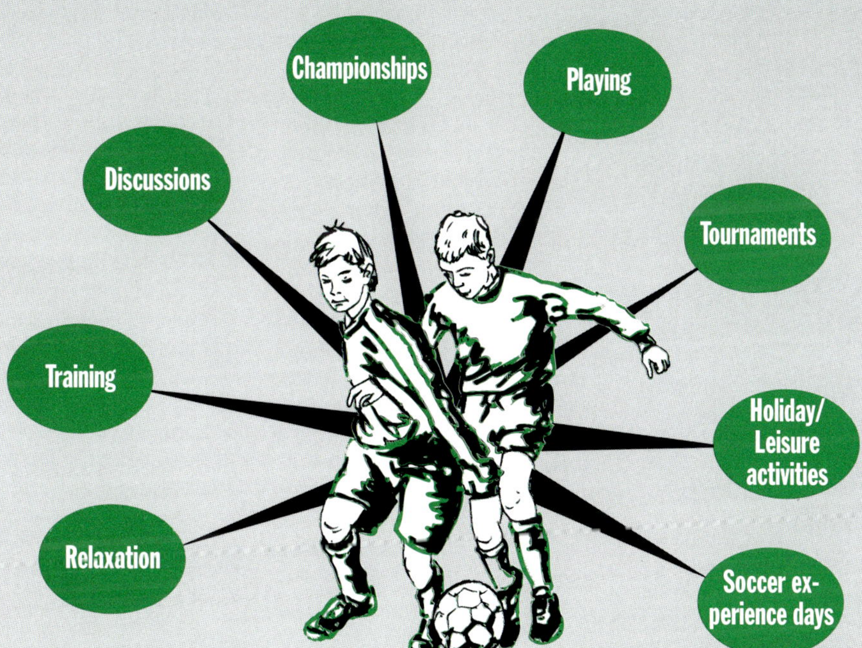

First comes soccer – but then...

Children and young people mainly join a soccer club in order to play soccer regularly and have a lot of fun doing just that. Most young players also want to compete with teams from other clubs as well as learn more about soccer. Consequently it is essential for clubs' youth department to 'pep up' all the training and playing activities they offer youngsters, especially by tailoring them to the respective age groups.

■ First and foremost children just want to **play** soccer. The young players want to have fun and give free reign to their natural urge to be active. This need is all the greater amongst today's children as their unrestricted "world of play and movement" is gradually shrinking.

■ The element of fun in actively playing soccer also remains the most important motive in subsequent age groups, although at this level the soccer played becomes more refined, as the young players seek to learn something and keep on fine-tuning their soccer skill.

■ So junior club players today are still very interested in doggedly, but attractively improving their personal soccer skills and regularly taking part in sporting competitions (i.e. playing league fixtures).

■ At the same time, however, the majority of youth players are looking for more from their club than just sport. During adolescence, there is also a growing desire for variety, social contact, relaxation, camaraderie, etc. connected with their sporting activities.

Children's soccer is booming at club level! Every season there are more and more F and E junior teams. In the older age groups, however, it is regrettable that far too many junior players then suddenly leave their clubs. A large number of clubs are finding it tremendously hard to put together teams in the B and A categories. There are – thank goodness – highly effective possibilities for countering this trend. However, new ideas and initiatives are required!

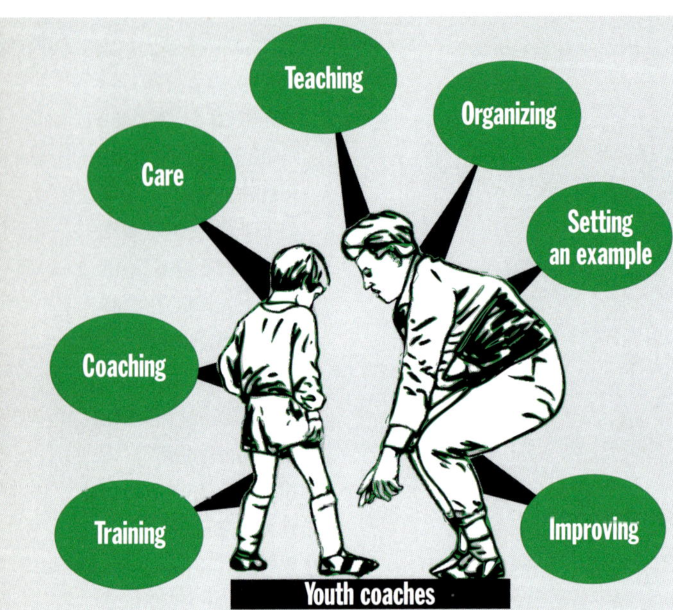

What is expected of youth coaches

■ **Training:** The best way of motivating youth players is to provide attractive training geared to the age group concerned. Training based simply on instinct is not sufficient!
Planning the training program in advance takes time, but to be a committed junior coach it simply has to be done.

■ **Coaching:** Trainers' duties will vary according to the age of the players concerned. The youngest age groups should only be given really essential instructions before or during the game using language that the children in question can easily understand. Otherwise, the trainer must consciously hold back while at the same time always being there to answer the youngsters' many questions and provide assistance. And remember the golden rule: praise, praise and more praise!

■ **Supervising:** Children need free space. For this reason, youth coaches definitely do not have to have each child 'under control' at all times, acting as a sort of 'chief supervisor'. Nor should they impose themselves, over-dramatize each triviality or protect their 'little ones' from every difficulty encountered. On the other hand, they must have a good feel of whether one of the children in their charge has real problems and needs help above and beyond the normal measure of care provided.

■ **Educating:** However, giving children space to try things out themselves is only one dimension. Every responsible junior coach also has to foster positive personal traits by offering some guidance to the children in their care.

Furthermore, any group can only function by sticking to certain behavioural patterns. This means that some basic rules have to be learned, concerning aspects such as punctuality, tidying up and asking permission to miss training or a game. The top educational objective remains that of teaching the youngsters to think and act independently and accept responsibility for their own actions. This process of growing into a state of extensive independence begins with giving children limited scope to act as they wish.

■ **Organizing:** The youth coaches area of responsibility usually extends beyond actual playing and training activities. Especially where they are provided with little relief by the other club officials (committee, youth leader), the youth coach has to take care of lots of things, e.g. finding a sponsor for shirts or organizing leisure activities and tournaments. However, the coaches time is limited. Active assistance from parents can help relieve this situation.

■ **Setting an example:** If coaches want to convey a positive attitude towards soccer and foster certain mental characteristics, they must also set an example themselves, i.e. being well-mannered, adopting a friendly approach, being fair, punctual, sporting and enthusiastic about playing soccer as well as showing respect and a sense of fair play vis-à-vis the opposing team and referee.

■ **Improving:** Many junior coaches draw their training activities solely from the range of exercises familiar to them from when they were still playing. This results in a completely inappropriate training structure. Youth training must never be a carbon copy of adult training. Even if it takes additional time, responsibly-minded junior coaches must acquire at least a basic knowledge of the modern training methods suited to the age groups concerned.

TIPS

How to make the activities offered by a soccer club more attractive

- **Soccer activities specially geared towards children and young people**
- **Flexible organization of fixtures**
- **Alternative forms of tournament (e.g. played on a small pitch)**
- **Organizing informal games**
- **Offering attractive additional activities that have nothing to do with sport**

Expectations of youth work in clubs

■ Children and young people still join soccer clubs mainly because they want to play soccer at a high, competitive level. However, in future such activities will have to be made more attractive and be more closely geared to the needs of the youngsters in question. Junior players must have fun and enjoy playing the game!

■ The tradition of playing matches at the weekend has to be adapted to the interests of junior players. For each age group category coaches should ask themselves whether the weekend is really the best and only possible time for league games.

■ Traditional league fixtures should be supplemented or even replaced by alternative types of tournament! Competitions played on small pitches are becoming increasingly popular. All the elements associated with a tournament afternoon result in a considerably higher level of communication and enjoyment.

■ The sporting interests of young people are often very diverse. Many youngsters shy away from organized training and games after a time and go. A decision like this – to leave their club – is not usually made from one day to the next. Irregular attendance at training – in conjunction with excuses made to the trainer and perhaps to oneself – is a first clear warning sign.

Trainers should not simply ignore such signs or punish players for not turning up without asking them why they failed to appear. Instead, they must at an early stage get together with the player, find out what the causes are and try to find solutions. The reasons for a sudden lack of interest can often be positively influenced by both the coach and club concerned, with the coach using his personality and/or taking appropriate action, structuring training in a different way or exploiting team morale.

■ Leaving the club should not be the only alternative to regular involvement in a competitive team, which places extremely high demands on people's time and self-discipline. Organizing regular but otherwise quite voluntary get-togethers for games played on the club's premises can offer a solution here. Both active and – in particular – temporarily passive junior club players can meet on such occasions for an informal kick-about. In this way, their contact with club soccer will not be broken off completely, they can return to the club at any time and making a come-back becomes much easier for them.

YOUTH WORK IN A SOCCER CLUB

SPORTING ACTIVITIES	NON-SPORTING ACTIVITIES
■ Interesting soccer training	■ Get-togethers for talks and discussions
■ Games geared towards children and youngsters	■ Day-trips, camping trips, holidays
■ Alternative types of soccer tournament	■ Parties/youth discos
■ Get-togethers for soccer matches played on club premises	■ Going to the cinema and theatre
■ Get-togethers for sport and play (additional sporting activities)	■ Cycling trips
	■ Other activities (e.g. anti-drugs campaign)

■ Soccer clubs will, in future, simply have to offer non-sporting leisure activities in addition to soccer training. Such activities provide players with opportunities for making social contacts, communicating, varying their activities and having fun. This does not mean in any way that the coach has to play the role of 'entertainer' in planning and organizing such additional activities. The youngsters should themselves be involved in doing this. Parents should also be motivated to help out with the younger age groups. In this way, youth players can experience first-hand that organizing life in the club is a responsibility that has to be shared by the club members themselves! This is the only way to develop lasting, true bonds of commitment within a club. It also encourages the youngsters to act with a sense of independence and responsibility. There is a wide range of non-sporting activities that juniors can be involved in, e.g. group holidays, day-trips, afternoons of games, cycling trips, camping trips, etc..

■ An interesting programme of playing and training activities and variety in the general day-to-day life of the club are fundamental elements of positive youth work. In addition, the attraction of playing soccer at club level, especially for children and young people, is strongly influenced by their personal contacts with team-mates and their coach. Individual players must feel 'comfortable and looked after' in the team. Coaches can contribute a great deal to positive team morale via their exemplary behaviour vis-à-vis individual players and the group as a whole, thereby conveying a sense of the fun and enjoyment associated with soccer within the club itself.

DEALING WITH YOUTH PLAYERS

TIP 1: Every youth player is an individual person in their own right, with all the relevant rights, entitlements and obligations that this implies. Players must therefore on no account have their minds made up for them, be 'mothered', offended or treated like 'machines' chasing goals, points and championships. Coaches must not just pay lip service to this important aspect of their relationship with the players by 'mouthing off' or making grandiose gestures. Instead, they must clearly recognize players' individuality in a variety of different situations and when dealing with them on a day-to-day basis.
Of course, youth trainers have the same rights themselves and should occasionally assert these firmly and consistently.

TIP 2: Youth coaches must not and cannot set their minds solely on playing the role of 'soccer expert'. Youth work in soccer must also fulfil valuable social and educational functions in today's world. However, to succeed in this, coaches need to have sufficient time, patience and understanding for the problems of their players both inside and outside the sporting domain (school, parents, friendships).

TIP 3: The basis of good personal contact between players and their coach is being able to talk positively. This talking must not be one-sided, e.g. with the coach simply issuing instructions, laying down rules or barking orders all the time and the junior players simply listening, asking questions and copying him the whole time. The players must be able to express their own thoughts, wishes, points of view and feelings in a lively exchange with the coach.
Such talks do not always work out. The coach and his players have to learn certain rules and patterns of conduct. Furthermore, a trusting relationship will take time to develop. It is important to be open with each other and this should start with the youngest age groups. Such openness must be practised, fostered and built on from the very outset.

TIP 4: Youth coaches must constantly be aware of their role-model function both with regard to sport and in human interaction in particular. They must set an example themselves of what they expect from their players by:

1. displaying their own enthusiasm for the game of soccer;

2. being well-mannered in their dealings with others, e.g. adopting a friendly and personal approach, showing a willingness to help, finding constructive solutions to conflicts and consciously seeking to support weaker players;

3. showing how to deal with victories and defeats in a positive way;

4. being 'genuine', i.e. not put on a front or playing certain roles.

CHAPTER 2

Basic training

OVERVIEW OF THE "BASIC TRAINING" SECTION

Teaching the basics using games specially suited to children

The first phase of training normally covers the 6-10 year-old age group. This is the age at which children join soccer clubs to learn how to play soccer from qualified specialists.
The main objective of this training phase can be summed up as "learning mobility – playing soccer".
The key here is to first teach the children the diverse basics of the game itself and its social and mental aspects which are essential when soccer is played as a team game:

- All-round powers of mobility and coordination (e.g. running, jumping, a sense of balance, reactions, a feel for rhythm)
- Basic technical skills and simple tactical moves
- A knowledge of the "minimum rules"
- How to behave in a group
- A sense of independence and feeling of individual responsibility.

To begin with, children in the youngest age groups should acquire these basic elements of the game largely of their own accord, by playing lots of informal games in small groups as well as taking part in agility games and performing any exercises that may be built into the training programme from time to time.
In this way, training will be fun right from the outset and the youngsters will enjoy themselves while they make progress. Remember, the first impression made by soccer training frequently determines the degree of further interest shown by many children later on. Acknowledgement of this makes the creation of an enjoyable, fun-filled atmosphere all the more important.

Soccer is not just fun when played in a club setting

As the "master of ceremonies", the coaches job is to create appropriate opportunities for playing and learning. He should organize soccer matches played in small groups at the beginning of the training session in such a way that all the children can join in to an equal extent. Although he must subsequently be there for everyone, he may only intervene when assistance is required. Coaches should also arrange additional games designed to boost the children's motivation by having them practise ball skills and put their agility to the test. More finely tuned soccer training can then commence at the end of the E junior stage, capitalizing on the previously acquired basic playing experience.

Small steps towards the objective – the 7-a-side game

The objective of basic training is to master the 7-a-side game (1 goalkeeper and 6 outfield players) by the end of this phase of training, which signals the transition to the D junior category.
To begin with, the youngest players are still unable to cope with the running about and skills required for the 7-a-side game. For this reason, F and E juniors have to be steered towards this objective progressively, by receiving training tailored to their particular age group and performance level. An excellent tool for doing this involves using the 4-a-side game.

OVERVIEW OF F AND E JUNIORS

TRAINING

Boys and girls at this age ...

■ just want to play.

■ often lack opportunities to expend their energy, as natural demands on their mobility and independent activities that used to be taken for granted (e.g. long walks to school) have waned considerably.

■ have increasingly less experience of playing soccer outside the club.

CONSEQUENCES

■ The first impression of soccer training can help to shape the child's continued interest in the sport and determine whether he wants to carry on.
As a result, training must be fun from the word go as well as guaranteeing progress.

■ Varied "training" can best be organized to take the form of plenty of games of soccer played in small teams.

■ Children also have to be familiarized with other possible movements, e.g. by taking part in running games.

PLAYING

Boys and girls at this age ...

■ want to compete with children their own age but do not ultimately attach great importance to the final result of the game. Defeats are quickly forgotten!

■ are fascinated just by the experience of playing the game and making progress. Children are happy and content when the games of soccer they play are geared especially to their capabilities. The result of the game is of only secondary importance.

CONSEQUENCES

■ Just like the types of game played in training, official fixtures must also be adapted to the level of the age group concerned because the youngest juniors cannot cope with the demands placed upon them by the 11-a-side game played by adults.

■ A steep learning curve and a high level of motivation can only be achieved by simplifying the game depending on the age of the players.

■ There should be no fixtures involving points or league tables for E and F juniors!

CARE

Boys and girls at this age ...

■ have – until they start school – only limited and "sheltered" social contact, which does not normally extend beyond their parents, brothers and sisters and a few neighbours and relatives.
At school, they then suddenly become just one individual amongst many, having to fit in, establish new relationships, deal with conflict situations, and so forth.

■ are often moody and have little self-confidence.

CONSEQUENCES

■ By playing their chosen sport, junior footballers must learn how to fit into a group, both on and off the playing field.

■ They must come to learn that common objectives can only be achieved if everybody helps everyone else and shares the workload.

■ The youngest players must ultimately learn that playing against each other also always involves playing with each other. The opposing team must be shown respect as a playing partner.

Focus on games played in small teams

Introducing 6 to 10 year-old children to the game of soccer must not be geared towards the requirements and kind of training associated with the adult game. It cannot be stated often enough: children's training must not simply resemble a scaled-down adult training programme!

Instead the training situation involving what for many youngsters constitutes their first intensive contact with soccer must comprise objectives and activities suited to the age group in question.

■ The clear focus of training for children must be directed on games played in small teams shooting into goals. This is because children learn soccer primarily by playing a lot. In this way, they will experience the fascination of the game in all its intensity – just like street football in the past. Their experiences at this stage form the basis for a longer-term, enduring motivation for playing football and therefore also for more positive developments within youth soccer itself. To achieve this, the demands of the 7-a-side competitive game can be reduced by:

- making the teams smaller,
- making the pitch smaller,
- making the rules simpler.

Doing any of these will make it easier for children to follow individual situations during play. The character of the game of football is not changed at any time. The children play "proper soccer" at all times - just as they wish.

■ The ideal game in this respect is 4-a-side shooting into goals as this is the most reduced format of the game which still includes all the technical and tactical elements featuring in the adult game. However, other team-games are of course also possible, such as 2-a-side or 3-a-side into goals. For the very young players, one entire training session a week should consist exclusively of games played in small teams as a single "playing unit".

■ The simple exercise of playing into two goals helps the children acquire the rudiments of the most important technical and tactical skills. This process of learning by playing is consolidated by motivating exercises involving basic elementary technical skills, i.e. dribbling, passing, shooting. These must be organized in such an interesting and varied way that they also encourage individual flair and creativity.

■ It is now generally accepted that all-round basic athletic training is absolutely essential for producing top-level performances later. Many youth players nowadays are nowhere near agile enough and move about clumsily and without any feel for bouncing, rolling or lofted balls.

The youngest players must therefore also improve their ball and agility skills, the so-called "qualities of coordination", simultaneously while training to play soccer. The more diverse and varied these additional training exercises are for the very young, the quicker they will learn to play soccer and the better they will be.

It is essential for coaches to provide this all-round basic training if the children are to be ideally prepared for playing the game of soccer. And if additional exercises and games are included in the training program, this will help the youngsters to master a wide range of movements.

Tackling is a key element in training and the game

TIPS ON TRAINING AND PLAYING 4-A-SIDE SOCCER

PITCH AND GOALS

The pitch normally measures 40 metres by 20 metres, though this has to be adapted to the age and capabilities of the players concerned.
For example, when the very youngest children play amongst themselves, it is more advisable to use smaller playing areas. Youth players must be able to follow the game and get involved at all times. The boundaries of the pitch are to be clearly marked with cones or something similar. The goals should be between 2 and 5 metres wide. The height of the goals will depend primarily on the markers used (e.g. the height of poles) but should not exceed 2 metres.

BALL

The soccerballs used must be suitable for children (i.e. not weigh more than 300 g) so as not to overtax the strength of the youngsters and to enable them to apply and develop "correct" techniques without any difficulty.

MINIMUM RULES

Children need only a few rules to play soccer. But it is important that they understand how the rules are applied. Nor do they need a referee, either! Instead they should settle any disputes amongst themselves simply and promptly to ensure that the game can continue as quickly as possible.

- **Teams should consist of 3 to 5 players. The basic formation is 4-a-side. However, to get everyone involved it is also possible to play 4-against-3, 5-against-4 or 5-a-side.**
- **A kick-off is used only at the very beginning of the game. So after a goal has been scored, the game is restarted with a goal kick!**
- **When the ball goes into touch, no throw-in is awarded. Instead, the ball is placed on the touchline and kicked back into play.**
- **Corner kicks are taken from the respective corner of the pitch.**
- **Any breach of the rules results in a direct free kick, whereby the players on the opposing team must be at least 3 metres away from the ball.**
- **There is no off-side rule.**

COACHING

These soccer matches played in small teams should be relatively carefree and informal for players in the F and E junior categories. From the D category upwards, however, the focus can be placed on specific key aspects of the game by using the many different variations of the 4-a-side game.

Why 4-a-side exactly?

4-a-side is a game format that fits in well with the carefree world of children's play and the street soccer of yesterday.
For children, it is at the same time attractive, eventful, exciting and productive in terms of learning.
The basis of the 4-a-side game is the clearly defined fundamental concept of the game of soccer, which is also easy for children to understand - namely, scoring goals and preventing goals.
The 4-a-side game conveys all the essential basic technical and tactical elements and objectives of the 11-a-side adult game in a playing environment that is easy to follow.
However, one major difference here is that the children are not over-stretched by being made to do too much running or play long passes.
In addition, the shorter distance between the goals means that young players can score more frequently and quickly, so that all-important sense of fulfilment builds up automatically. All the children are involved in attack and defence at almost every stage of the game. The small size of the teams makes helping each other an absolute necessity.

Advantages of the 4-a-side game

▶ Soccer matches played in small teams with goals guarantee exciting, enjoyable and – from the learning point of view – effective training for children and youth players.

▶ A further feature of the 4-a-side game is that it constitutes the smallest framework in which all the basic situations and elementary technical/tactical elements of "grown-up" soccer occur and can be improved through training.

▶ The 4-a-side game can be played in all age groups, regardless of the children's or youngsters' level of training and development. This makes it possible to plan a schedule of fixtures that is entertaining and varied for all concerned.

▶ Later on in life, youth soccer players find it relatively easy to apply the technical and tactical skills they have previously learnt to the 11-a-side game.

▶ The 4-a-side game presents possibilities for training children on all the features of attractive and forward-looking play, e.g. deliberate build-ups, creative individual moves, adventurous and original attacking moves and enthusiastic, unified defensive play designed to win back possession of the ball as quickly as possible with a view to launching a counter-attack.

INTERESTING, SIMPLE TRAINING

WITH 2 TEAMS

- **The best solution for 6 to 10 players is a game with two teams shooting into 2 goals.**
- **Games should last no longer than 10 to 15 minutes.**
- **Before a new game begins, a "motivating game" or agility/ball-skill exercise can be included for "loosening up" purposes.**
- **The teams can be re-selected between the individual games.**

WITH 3 TEAMS

- **The following simple but interesting and efficient arrangement is suitable for a situation in which there are 3 teams:**
2 teams play 4-a-side (each game lasts 10 minutes) while the team not playing is kept busy doing exercises and playing games designed to improve their:
1. Soccer technique
2. Ball skills
3. Agility.
- **Which team are the "champions" when all the teams have played one another?**

WITH 4 TEAMS

- **A 4-a-side tournament played on two parallel pitches is ideal for 4 teams.**
1st round:
Pitch A: team 1 - team 2
Pitch B: team 3 - team 4
2nd round:
Pitch A: team 1 - team 3
Pitch B: team 2 - team 4
3rd round:
Pitch A: team 2 - team 3
Pitch B: team 1 - team 4
Which team are the champions at the end?
- **Where particular "building blocks" are also to be taught, on top of simply playing informal games of soccer, training may be organized as follows:**
Two teams play soccer against each other while the other two teams practice/play supervised by the trainer. They then switch around.

WITH INDIVIDUAL ASSESSMENT

- **As many pitches are laid out as are required for all the players to be able to play at once.**
- **Five games are played simultaneously over a period of 10 minutes. The teams are completely reshaped after each game.**
- **Each player can improve his personal points tally in every game using the following points system:**
10 points for a win
5 points for a draw
1 point for each goal scored by his team.
Which player has the most points by the end?

The importance of preparing the training program

Training programs for F and E juniors, in particular, must be prepared with specific objectives in mind.
All too often, training is based merely on coaches' 'instincts'. Many junior coaches develop their training programs pretty much as they go along, holding to a certain routine. In so doing, they merely draw on their own repertoire of exercises, learned during their soccer playing career.
However, training kids is by no means 'child's play', and on no account may it simply be a carbon copy of adult training either! Accordingly, trainers who want to get the very best out of their youngest juniors have no alternative but to prepare their training sessions with the utmost care.

Questions before putting together a training program

When preparing a training program, every coach must ask himself certain questions and then incorporate the answers into his planning.

Objectives:

- What do I want to achieve in today's training session?

Content:

- Which exercises and games are the best ones to use to achieve these objectives?
- Will the kids enjoy them enough?
- Are they suitably geared to the children's ability?
- Can they be easily explained and understood?
- Is all the necessary playing and training equipment available?
- How can the players themselves help me?
- What is too difficult for them?
- Is there a smooth transition between the individual parts of the training session and organizational aspects?
- How can everything best be cleared away at the end of the session?
- How can I kick off the training session in such a way that the players can 'give their all' right from the word go?
- Is the available training area sufficient for the games and exercises envisaged?

Fundamental principles of training

Coaches also have to take account of a number of fundamental principles of training. It is particularly important that these be applied with players belonging to the youngest age groups, because this will maximize the 'fun factor' and enable the kids to make optimum progress.

Training exercises must be adapted to the varying capabilities of the players involved

The level of ability of F and E youth teams often differs considerably. Indeed, the youngest age groups often include players ranging from 'little experts' to beginners whose performance levels lag way behind those of the former. If this is the case, divide the players up accordingly into different groups and set them training exercises which match their individual level of skill. This is the only way to prevent them from being either over or under-stretched. Coaches should aim to ask a great deal of their players, but not the impossible. Otherwise the children will be disappointed, stop enjoying their training and tend to disrupt the session for others.
So you see, training kids is by no means 'child's play'! Flexibility is an important quality for any trainer, especially when coaching the youngest age groups. However, even the most committed trainers do run up against certain limitations.
For this reason, splitting the children into different groups on the basis of their ability will become much easier if the trainer can fall back on an assistant. A suitable person for this job can normally be found amongst the children's parents or the club's older youth teams, but always pick someone who is genuinely interested in taking on the task.

Make sure that the players feel they have really achieved something as often as possible

Children's concentration and enthusiasm for training can best be increased by combining training exercises with mini competitions.
Children want to compete with others and display their own ability in a direct comparison with their

TRAINING DURING THE WEEK

1ST TRAINING SESSION

- Games and exercises designed to improve ball skills
- Games and exercises designed to improve the players' agility
- Informal games of soccer: 4-a-side into goals (possibly in the form of a tournament)

2ND TRAINING SESSION

- Motivational soccer games focusing on some of the key elements of the game:
  - dribbling
  - shooting
  - passing, ball control
  - heading
  - tackling
- To finish up with: Soccer matches played in small teams into goals

COMPETITIVE GAMES

- 7-a-side league games on a half-size pitch (but do without league tables or championships where F and E juniors are concerned)
- Development of new forms of competition (e.g. 4-a-side tournament afternoons)

peers. Nothing shores up a child's still under-developed self-confidence more than the taste of success in a sporting competition.

There is no substitution for a child's sense of achievement at being faster than his peers, at having scored the most goals or points or won a lot of tackles, etc.; accordingly trainers must give them the opportunity to feel successful as often as possible, by setting the players appropriate exercises. After all, success will give the players the courage to take on and master even more difficult tasks.

Obviously, the greatest sense of achievement when playing soccer is gained by scoring a goal. For this reason, almost all training exercises should give the players a chance to shoot at goal and incorporate a competition to crown a 'top goalscorer'.

Whatever happens, coaches must not neglect to give the results of these competitions - feedback is extremely important for children of this age. Indeed, young players will expect the goal totals to be totted up and to receive praise from their trainer when they perform well ("well done", "great stuff"). They will also expect to receive recognition when they try something courageous, even if it does not quite come off.

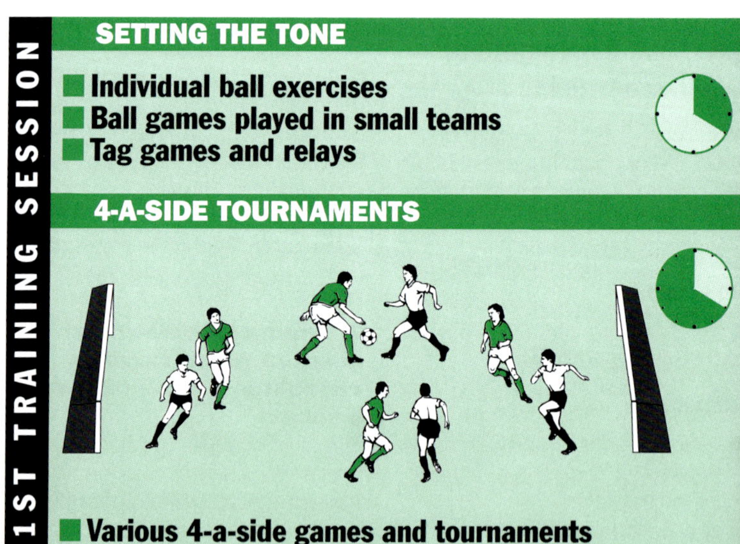

In soccer matches played in small teams it is important that everyone has a chance to win!

The main focus of F and E juniors' training must be on games of soccer played in small teams.

Here too, it is essential that all the youngsters have a chance to feel the greatest possible sense of achievement. By picking teams carefully and introducing a few 'special rules', the dominance of strong players can be reduced whenever required and children with less natural ability can be given more space. However, the sense and purpose of such special rules must be explained to the children right at the outset. This is because children of this age have a very pronounced sense of fairness.

By picking teams cleverly and introducing additional rules when required, differences in ability can be ironed out to give all the teams an equal chance of winning:

■ Teams comprising children of equal ability play each other on different pitches.

■ A team of 'weaker' children is pitted against a smaller team of stronger players (3 against 2, 4 against 3, etc.).

■ Mixed teams, comprising equal numbers of talented and less talented children, play against each other.

■ Here are some examples of rules preventing individual high-ability players from dominating the match as 'solo entertainers':

1. Goals scored by certain weaker players are made to count double
2. Free kicks/penalties are taken only by weaker players
3. Every player in a team must score a goal.

2ND TRAINING SESSION

SETTING THE TONE

- **Individual ball exercises**
- **Ball games played in small teams**
- **Tag games and relays**

MOTIVATIONAL SOCCER GAMES

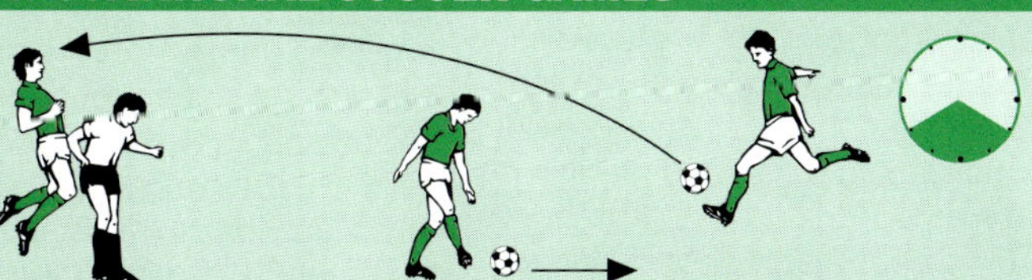

CONCLUDING GAME

- **Various 4-a-side games and tournaments**

Tips on training units

▶ In the **first training unit** of the week, after the tone has been set the children must be given a chance to just play. The maxim here is 'learn to play...by playing'!

▶ 4-a-side games played into goals are the best way of achieving this.

▶ Trainers should not intervene. Learning by playing offers boys and girls a chance to put their own ideas into practice. Children must be allowed to develop their game freely.

▶ The **second training unit** of the week should include additional games of football designed to provide motivation and teach individual aspects of technique in a deliberate, playful way geared to the children in question.

▶ Unlike the older age groups later on, F and E juniors do not need any specific warm-up program at the beginning of each training session.

In this age group the 'warm-up' simply involves 'getting going', i.e. allowing the kids to expend a lot of energy while having some fun. Beginning training sessions in this way quickly satisfies the youngest children's initial craving for action and makes it easier to organize the soccer matches played in small teams during the brief 'quiet phase' that follows.

▶ Individual games should not last more than 15 minutes, since children of this age still lack the ability to concentrate for longer periods.

Whenever necessary, short breaks for a drink can be taken between individual exercises, giving the

ORGANIZATIONAL AIDS

TIP 1: The numbers of children in the training group often prevent the formation of teams of equal size the whole time. If so, it is quite alright to play 3 against 4 or 4 against 5 (on separate pitches).
Coaches can exploit differences in team sizes to compensate for differences in the teams' respective levels of ability.

TIP 2: Whenever organizing games between teams of equal size, i.e. playing 3-a-side or 4-a-side and leaving left-over players within the group, coaches can opt for the following solutions to involve the latter:

- **Allow a substitute to one team (and after each goal bring on the player left on the bench).**
- **Have one team defend a bigger goal and also include a goalkeeper (with the goalkeeper substituted after each goal has been scored).**

TIP 3: The youth players should be able to follow the run of play at all times. So the teams' strips should be as distinct as possible and care should be taken to mark the boundaries of the pitch as clearly as possible (cones).

TIP 4: Any available goals should be used (handball goals, 5-metre-wide goals). The biggest thrill for youth players is to shoot into a 'real' goal.

youngsters a chance for some refreshment and to 'switch off' for a while.

▶ The groups of players should be repeatedly picked afresh, but coaches should always ensure that the teams are as evenly matched as possible.

▶ The motivational exercises designed to train youngsters to improve basic aspects of their elementary soccer technique should not be geared towards making them perfect the sequences of skills concerned. To begin with, all the youngsters need to do is familiarize themselves with the rudiments of basic technique and find their own way of dealing with the ball. The trainer should only give occasional assistance where there are obvious difficulties.

Tips on indoor training

Coaches of younger age groups will have to revert to indoor training for a substantial part of the season (from roughly November to March). This need not be a disadvantage for the youngest players' playing and training - on the contrary, indoor training provides an ideal setting for some of the main aspects of basic training:

① The frequent games played in small teams, which are easier for the children to follow, can also be organized indoors without any problems.

② The ball can be played off the walls, facilitating exciting games without constant interruptions.

③ Exercises focusing on aspects of technique are not disrupted by bumpy ground or adverse weather conditions.

④ Equipment normally used for other indoor sports can be used to set up interesting exercises designed to teach the youngsters basic aspects of coordination.

On the other hand, indoor training makes greater demands on the coaches organizational skills, because the available training area is normally much smaller than it would be outside.

So here are a few useful tips for organizing efficient training indoors:

▶ At the beginning, it is essential that all the players can really 'get into' the training session straight away. Coaches would therefore be well-advised to avoid long-winded explanations or difficult exercises at the start of sessions.

Once the youngsters have been allowed to let off some steam, they will be much better able to face any breaks in the action that may be necessary.

▶ Two or even three pitches for soccer matches played in small teams (ranging from 1-on-1 to 3-a-side) can also be marked out indoors, but they should always be clearly separated from each other (use benches, boxes, etc.). In this way a large number of kids will be able to play at the same time.

▶ Where games are played in bigger teams, the groups not involved should be given additional tasks (e.g. serving as outlets for return passes on the touchline).

▶ Indoor sports equipment can be used relatively easily to organize interesting circuit training!

CONTENTS OF BASIC TRAINING

AGILITY

Diverse additional activities designed to promote all-round athleticism as a basis for optimizing players' performance during soccer matches:

- Relays
- Tag games
- Exercises with other sports equipment

EXERCISES AND GAMES

BALL SKILLS

Diverse additional activities designed to promote all-round ball skills as a basis for optimizing players' performance during soccer matches:

- Individual exercises with the ball
- Exercises in pairs
- Ball games played in small groups

EXERCISES AND GAMES

4-A-SIDE

- Soccer matches played in small teams into goals, an essential component of F and E youth training
- Carefree, informal games intended to provide initial soccer experience and be fun
- Allowing the kids to learn by simply playing soccer
- Building up their long-term motivation to play soccer

TECHNIQUE

Interesting exercises for additional training of elementary soccer techniques

- Dribbling
- Passing
- Shooting/heading

MOTIVATIONAL SOCCER GAMES

1-ON-1

Tackling exercises for additional training in 1-on-1 situations, the most important basic situation in soccer

- 1-on-1 into one goal
- 1-on-1 into two goals
- 1-on-1 as a team competition

MOTIVATIONAL SOCCER GAMES

RUNNING GAMES AND RELAYS

The various forms of running (involving sudden changes of direction or pace, beginning from different starting positions, etc.) constitute players basic form of mobility. It is therefore essential to include interesting running games in the standard training programme set for beginners.

Return shuttle relay

Each group lines up behind a starting line.
Cones are placed 2 metres and 5 metres in front of the group.
The first runner sprints to the first cone, touches it briefly with one hand and sprints back to the starting line. He then immediately runs to the second cone and back, before sending the next player off with a tap of his hand.
Which team is the first to finish?

Variants:

- Each player has to run twice (or three times).
- The players are made to *run around* each cone.
- The next player in the group stands waiting with his legs spread wide apart. The returning runner has to crawl through his legs before sending the new runner on his way.
- The runners are made to perform a small additional exercise at each cone (e.g. briefly lying down on their stomach or back).

Chain relay

Groups made up of a maximum of four players are formed. The groups line up approximately 5 metres in front of a marker indicating a turning point. The first runner runs alone around the turning point and back to the group, then takes the next player by the hand and the two of them set off to run around the turning point, pick up the third player, and so on.
When the entire group has run around the turning point, they continue the exercise, but this time dropping off one runner at the starting point each time, starting with the first runner. The game ends when the last runner has run the last leg alone.

Return relay in pairs

Groups of three are formed. Two players from each group run around a turning point holding hands while the third player waits at the start. When the pair returns, one player is dropped of and the waiting team mate joins in the next leg, and so on.
Which group is the first to complete two (or three) rounds?

The distance to the turning point must be suited to the age of the children involved. Make sure that the youngsters can run the course at full speed.

Transporting balls

Both groups line up behind the starting line. Two collecting points are marked on the course using cones, poles, or some other suitable markers. Some balls are placed ready at one collecting point while the other is empty.
The players take it in turns to run to a ball, carry it to the second collecting point and then send off the next runner with a tap of the hand.
Which group is the first to transfer all the balls to the second collecting point?

NB: Other items can be used instead of balls (e.g. cones, soccer shirts, etc.).

Shuttle relay with additional tasks

Two groups belonging to the same team line up opposite each other for a shuttle relay. The runners must perform a forward roll while running to the other side.
Which is the first group to reach the original starting position?

Variants:

- Incorporation of a backward roll
- Incorporation of a full turn.
- Each team member has to briefly lie on his stomach or back on the way to the other side.
- Each team member has to jump over certain obstacles (balls, cones).
- Each team member has to run a slalom course (poles, cones).

Return relay with additional tasks

The groups line up for a return relay. A roughly 5-metre section is marked out in the middle of the course, e.g. using cones. Each team member has to perform a particular task in this section on his way to the turning point (e.g. crawl, hop). On the way back, he may run back directly to his group

Variant:

- Each team member has to perform the same (or another) task on their way back.

Shuttle relay

The players stand in two groups (of equal size where possible) behind markers approximately 10 to 15 metres apart. The leading players are given the order to run to the other end, where they send off their opposing numbers with a tap of the hand.

Which is the first team to have all its players back in the original starting position?

Variants:

- Each player has to run 2 (3) legs before the shuttle relay is completed.
- The next runner stands waiting with his legs wide apart. The player running towards him must first crawl through his legs before the next runner can start.

Return relay

The players in the individual groups line up approximately 10 metres in front of their respective turning marker (cone, pole, etc.). On the word go, the leading runners run around the turning point as fast as they can and then send of the next player with a tap of the hand. He then also sprints off, turning around the marker, and so on.

Which group is the first to finish?

Variants:

- Each player has to run 2 (3) legs.
- The players each start from different positions (e.g. squatting, sitting with their legs stretched out in front of them, lying on their back).

TAG GAMES

Especially in the youngest age groups, games of tag are an ideal way of teaching and consolidating basic agility skills in a playful manner: e.g. starting and stopping, making sudden changes of direction, feinting and dodging, hopping, jumping! Games of tag should therefore be regularly included in the warm-up stage of the training session.

Tag

Depending on the size of the group, between one and three players are picked to be "it" (and identified using, say, team sashes). The player who is tagged then trades with the person catching him. Who got tagged the fewest number of times within a set time?

Variants:

- Players who are "it" and runners have to hop on one leg, hop on two legs, crawl on all fours, etc.
- Roles do not change after being tagged. Which player when "it" can catch the most players within a fixed period of time? New players are then picked to be "it" for the next session of the game.

Amusing tag game

The same as before, except that the tagged runner, as the new player picked to be "it", may stipulate how all the other players have to move around (running, hopping, etc.).

Variant:

- The coach sporadically calls out instructions on how the players must move around.

Timed tag

One player is made "it" for a fixed period of time (15 to 30 seconds). Tagged players immediately drop into a squatting position. A new player is then picked to be "it". Which player achieves the greatest number of tags?

Double tag

The players form pairs, holding each other's hand and moving around within a limited space.
A pair picked to be "it" first chases the other pairs, trading roles with another pair only when the tag is carried out correctly, i.e. without letting go of each other's hand.
Which pair is tagged the least number of times over a set period?

Variants:

- One pair is picked to be "it" for a fixed time. Tagged pairs immediately drop into a squatting position. Which pair tags the highest number of other pairs?
- Which pair was the quickest to tag all the other pairs?
- All pairs have to hop on one leg.

Marker tag

Markers are set up within a certain area.
One player is made "it" and chases the other players, who can save themselves by running to a marker where they cannot be tagged.
Only one player can take refuge at a particular marker at any one time. Whenever a second player arrives at an already occupied marker, the player already there must leave immediately. Which catcher achieves the most tags in 1 minute.

Line tag

Two (or three) players are picked to be "it" and line up on the base line of the pitch. The other players wait on the opposite base line as runners.
On the word "go", the runners have to try to reach the other base line without being tagged by the approaching players trying to catch them. When a players who is "it" tags a runner, the two swap roles. As soon as all the players have reached their starting positions, the word "go" is given again.
Which player can break through to the line on the other side the most times within a set period (or in 10 run-throughs, for example)?

Call tag

The players form pairs, with one player in each pair being allocated the number 1 and the other the number 2.
All the players run around freely in a marked-out space.
When a number is called (1 or 2), that player must then try to tag his partner within 10 seconds, after which a new number is called out.
1 point is awarded for each successful tag.
Which player has scored the most points after 10 heats?

HOW THE TAG GAME WORKS

"Day and night"

Teams 1 and 2 line up facing each other 2 to 4 metres apart. Base lines are marked out about 20 metres behind each team. The coach calls out one of the numbers. The players belonging to the team corresponding to the called-out number then try to reach their base line as quickly as possible. The players of the other team chase them and tag as many as possible before they run across the base line. Everyone then goes back to their starting positions. Tagged players score 1 minus point. Which team has the least number of minus points after 10 run-throughs (after 10 minutes)?

DAY AND NIGHT

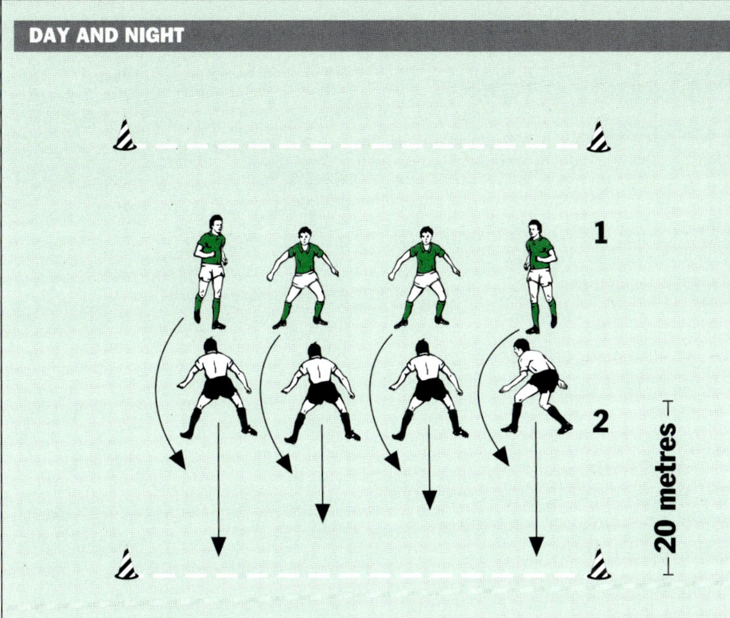

Variant:

- The players must start from different positions (e.g. squatting, lying on their stomachs).

N.B.:

- Tag games must be organized in such a way that everybody is actively involved. Avoid a situation in which players are quick to be eliminated from the game.
- Where the groups are too large, the players should be divided up over two or three playing areas.

HOW THE TAG GAME WORKS

Tag relay

The players in Group A wait in a defined area as runners. Group B players are "it" and start from a marker placed outside the area. The first player who is "it" tries to tag a player as quickly as possible. The tagged player is then eliminated. With a tap of the hand, the player who is "it" passes on the mantle, sending the next member of his team into the area to be "it". Which team can tag all the players on the opposing team in the shortest time?

TAG RELAY

Variants:

- Tagged players stay in the defined area. Which group of players can make the highest number of tags within two (three) minutes?
- The same, but in the form of "double tag", i.e. the runners and catchers move about in pairs holding hands.

INDIVIDUAL EXERCISES WITH THE BALL

Interesting training exercises with rolling, bouncing and lofted balls must be included in each training session (especially in the warm-up) and be suitable for children. The ball should not always only be played with the foot. The most important thing is for the youngest players to familiarize themselves thoroughly with the ball as a piece of games equipment.

Preliminary dribbling exercises

All the players have a ball and move around freely.

■ They dribble while changing direction as often as possible.

■ They dribble
- only with their right foot,
- only with their left foot,
- only with the outside of the foot (photo 1),
- alternating between their right and left feet.

■ The players dribble the ball in a tight circle, big circle or figure of eight.

■ The players dribble the ball, making brief, frequent contact with it.

■ The players dribble at high speed (changing direction frequently). The ball must be under control all the time (photo 2).

■ While dribbling, the players drag the ball back with the sole of the foot and then continue dribbling it forwards with the outside of the same foot. After a few metres they repeat the exercise:
- with the same foot,
- with the other foot,
- alternating between their right and left feet.

■ The players place the sole first of their right foot then of their left foot on the ball in quick succession, moving lightly on their feet.

■ The players nudge the ball forwards alternating between their right and left instep and then immediately drag it back towards their body with the sole of the foot (photo 3).

Photo 1

Photo 2

Photo 3

Bouncing the ball like in basketball

All the players have a ball which they bounce while moving around freely amongst each other. The following exercises are only suitable for training on a flat, even surface, otherwise the ball will bounce too unpredictably.

■ Bouncing the ball
- ... while hopping on one leg.
- ... with an occasional full rotation of the body.
- ... while running backwards.
- ... while jumping up and down on the spot.
- ... while running sideways.
- ... with their eyes closed briefly.
- ... on the spot – at the same time the players adopt particular postures when instructed (squatting, sitting, standing on one leg, kneeling, dropping to a press-up position). Who can do this without interrupting their bouncing of the ball?
- ... on the move – the players have to briefly touch the ground with a particular part of their body while the ball is bouncing.
- ... alternately with their right and left hands.
- ... as low/high as possible.

■ Two players hold each other's hand while each bounces a ball with their other hand. Both players switch hands when so instructed.

■ Two players bounce the ball while standing back to back. At the sound of the whistle they each make a half-turn and continue bouncing their partner's ball.

Kicking the ball up in the air

Each player has a ball. The players spread out so as not to get in each other's way. The coach must be able to watch them all at the same time.

■ The players let the ball drop a short way out of their hands and then kick it back up with their left or right instep, catching it immediately.
■ The same as before, except the ball is allowed to bounce once before it is caught.
■ The players drop the ball from their hands and play it twice with their right or left instep before catching it again.
■ The players first juggle the ball twice, then let it bounce once and juggle it again twice with their right or left instep. Only then do they catch the ball.
■ The players kick the ball into the air, squat briefly and then catch the ball.
Variants: lying on their stomach, full rotation of the body.
Which players also manage the difficult exercises?
■ The players kick the ball into the air, let the falling ball bounce off their thigh (chest, head) and catch it again.
■ The players juggle the ball for as long as possible with all the parts of the body allowed in the rules of soccer (foot, head, thigh). Who can keep going the longest?
■ The players juggle the ball using only the part of their body they are instructed to use (e.g. their foot, thigh, etc.). Who is best at this?

Juggling the ball with the instep

Juggling the ball with the head

Throwing the ball in the air and catching it

Each player has a ball. The players spread out so as not to be in each other's way.

■ The players throw the ball into the air from various starting positions (squatting, sitting, kneeling, lying on their stomachs or backs) and then jump up and catch the ball.
Who can do the most in 30 seconds?
■ The players throw the ball into the air from a standing position and catch it in different positions, e.g. kneeling, sitting, lying down.
■ The players throw the ball into the air and perform one of the following additional tasks before catching the ball again:
touch the ground with both hands, make a full rotation of the body, jump and make a full rotation, clap their hands behind their backs, do a forward roll, squat down, lay on their stomachs, etc.
Which players can manage the most difficult additional exercises?
Weaker players can be allowed to let the ball bounce once before catching it.
■ All the players line up on the touchline. The idea is to see who can get the ball to the other side of the pitch with the smallest number of throws. Players may not run with the ball in their hands.

SMALL-SIDED GAMES

Ball games played in small teams are a useful addition to soccer practice. They help to improve agility with the ball (even when pressurized by players on the opposing team). Such games can also help, in a playful way, to teach and consolidate basic tactical patterns that are important when playing soccer (e.g. positional play, teamwork, running into space).

Rebounding ball

In the gym, two groups play 6-a-side (5-a-side) handball into two basketball baskets. The aim of the game is to throw the ball against the ring or the board so that it bounces back onto the floor of the playing area (= 1 point for the attacking group).
The opposing group can prevent points being scored by catching the ball when it bounces back down but before it hits the ground.
Depending on the size of the teams, the game should last between 5 and 10 minutes.

Variants:

■ The attacking group is awarded two points if a team-mate catches the ball when it bounces back before it hits the ground.
■ The same group is awarded three points when the player throwing the ball catches it.
■ To encourage running into space as well as team play, the players are not allowed to take more than three steps with the ball.
■ Big differences in the level of ability between individual players or teams can be compensated for by awarding special points, for example.
Example for weaker teams:
Each throw hitting the basketball board counts as a point. The attacking group is awarded as many as three points for each basket.
■ If the difference in the teams' level of ability is too great, the coach can also join in, giving the weaker team an extra player.

Box basketball

In the gym, two groups play 6-a-side (7-a-side) handball into two basketball baskets.
Two small boxes are set up close to the baskets at both ends with two attackers standing on top of them. Only the players on the boxes, who regularly change places with the others, are allowed to score points.

Variants:

■ Only one box is set up for each basket.
■ All the players can score points but baskets scored by the players on the box count double.
■ Where there are big differences in ability, the weaker team plays with two players on the box, the stronger team with only one. Alternatively, the boxes of the weaker team are made higher, making it easier for them to score baskets.

Throw-in game

The pitch is divided into three zones of equal size. A group of four to six players lines up in each zone. The two teams in the off-field zones have balls and try to hit the players in the middle zone with proper soccer throw-ins. The only way the players in the middle zone can protect themselves from being hit is through skilful dodging or by catching the ball. Balls that remain in the middle are rolled back to the nearest off-field zone.
After four minutes, one of the groups from the off-field zones goes into the middle, and so on. Which group is hit the least number of times?

Variants:

■ If necessary, the middle zone can be made larger or smaller.
■ Players leave the pitch after being hit. Who is the last player left in the middle?

Piggy in the middle

On a playing area of about 10 x 10 metres, four attackers standing in the corners throw the ball to each other in such a way that the defender in the middle (the "piggy") cannot get to it. Where the "piggy" manages to get to the ball (touching it is sufficient), he trades places with the player whose pass he intercepted. If the ball drops to the ground or rolls outside the playing area while being passed between the outside players, the person responsible also trades places with the "piggy".

Variant:

■ The attackers are also allowed to bounce-pass the ball.

HOW THE BALL GAME WORKS

Chasing the runner

Two equally strong teams of six to 10 players are formed. Group A has a soft ball and is the "chasing team" within a defined playing area. Group B sends two players alternately onto the field as "runners". The "runners" can decide for themselves how long they want to stay on. The "chasing team" tries to hit as many "runners" as possible with the ball. A maximum of three steps is allowed while carrying the ball.
After about five minutes, the teams switch around.

Variants:

- The size of the playing area must be adapted to the size of the group and the ability of the players.
- No running with the ball is allowed.
- The "chasing team" is given a second ball.
- For larger groups, three "runners" can be sent onto the field at the same time.
- Only "indirect hits" are allowed, i.e. the ball has to bounce after being thrown.

HOW THE BALL GAME WORKS

Bouncing ball

In a defined playing area, two teams that are as evenly matched as possible play 5-a-side (4-a-side/6-a-side) handball into two goals without goalkeepers.
The idea is for the teams to score goals against each other using team-play.
However, only "indirect throws" are permitted as passes or shots. This means the ball has to bounce before being caught by a team-mate or crossing the goal line.

Variants:

- Players may not run more than three steps while carrying the ball.
- The players may not run with the ball at all, i.e. it must be played immediately.
- Circles are marked in front of both goals and the players are forbidden to enter them.
- The size of the goals and the playing area can be tailored to the ability of the players.

N.B.:

- The same precept as ever applies to the planning and playing of these games: make sure that the children gain the greatest possible sense of success.

DRIBBLING

The players should gradually learn to dribble the ball with more and more control, i.e. closer to their feet. At the same time, they should increasingly start to take their eyes off the ball, so as to follow the overall situation on the pitch at all times.

Dribbling using the front end of the foot

Dribbling with the inside of the foot

Dribbling with the outside of the foot

Tunnel soccer

All the players have a ball which they dribble in a defined area.
The coach moves around the pitch at a relaxed pace. The players watch and follow him while dribbling. From time to time, the coach stops and forms a "tunnel" by placing his feet wide apart. The players then play their own ball through the front end of the tunnel as quickly as possible.
The first three (four, five) players who manage to do this are awarded a point. The coach then sets off again.
Which player has the most points after a set time?

Variants:

- A number of obstacles are set up (e.g. cones or clubs) around which the players must dribble the ball while following the coach. Anyone knocking over an obstacle is awarded a minus point.
- For larger groups, a second "tunnel" can be formed by a spare player.

Pitch switching

Two playing areas are marked out about 15 metres apart. All the players are given a ball and dribble freely amongst each other on one of the two pitches. When the signal is given, they switch to the second playing area as quickly as possible in the following way: If the coach raises only one arm, the players dribble directly onto the other pitch. If he raises both arms simultaneously, they first have to dribble the ball round one of the two rear marker cones before switching.
The last player to reach the other pitch has to perform an additional task (e.g. sprinting to one of the marker cones and back).

Variants:

- With points: the first three players are awarded one point each. Which player has the most points after four to six games?
- The players have to perform an additional task with the ball (e.g. a full turn with the ball) on their way to the other pitch.
- Poles are used to set up a goal 3 metres wide between the two pitches. All the players have to dribble the ball through this goal to get to the other pitch.
- The players move around in the space between the two pitches. When the coach gives a hand signal, they sprint onto the selected playing area.
- The players are given various additional tasks while dribbling inside the playing area, e.g. dribbling the ball while making as many changes of direction as possible.

"Crab" soccer

The players are divided into two groups of equal size. The players in one group each have a ball while the others move around on all fours like crabs, as in "sit-down soccer".
The task of the "crabs" is to get balls away from the players' feet. The players on the ball dodge them by skilful dribbling. When a

"crab" wins the ball, the two players immediately trade places. Who was a "crab" least often over the 5 minutes?

Variants:

■ Only three or four players are "crabs" at the beginning, while the others dribble the ball around in the playing area. Any player losing his ball also becomes a "crab". Who is the last player left?
■ The players in a set group of "crabs" can only move up and down a half-way line marked between two base lines. The players in the other group each have a ball and try to dribble from one base line to the other as often as possible. If a "crab" touches a ball, the player who has been caught must go back to the starting position. Which player has achieved the most breakthroughs after a set period of time?
The two groups then switch around.

"Find the empty goal"

Five small goals are set up on a defined playing area using cones. Four of the goals are "manned", only the fifth one is empty. All the other players have a ball which they dribble around in the playing area.
When the signal is given, all four goalkeepers switch positions as quickly as possible and position themselves in one of the other goals.
The other players then have to play their ball as quickly as possible through the one small goal that has become empty. The first five players to do so are each awarded a point. All the players then continue dribbling the ball around for a while until the signal is given for the goalkeepers to change positions again.

"Stop dribbling" hand signal

The players each dribble a ball around amongst each other within a defined playing area. The coach and one player stand in diagonally opposite corners of the playing area.
From time to time, the coach or the other player raises a hand and the players on the pitch have to stop the ball as quickly as possible with the sole of their foot.
The player who is last to comply has to perform a previously determined additional task, such as doing three press-ups or sprinting around a marker and back.
The player in question then immediately changes places with the player in the corner and the game is restarted.

Variants:

■ The players have to stop the ball when the hand signal is given, leave it on the ground, then sprint round a pitch marker and back to their ball. Which player is the last to return?
■ While dribbling, the players have to stop the ball with their knee.
■ While dribbling, the players have to sit on the ball briefly.

Basketball tap

Apart from two (three) players who are "it", all the players dribble a ball around amongst each other within a defined playing area.
The players who are "it" bounce the ball, like in basketball, and have to tap the players who are dribbling, using their hand. Whenever they manage to make contact, the players concerned trade places. Which player was "it" least often after three minutes?

Variant:

■ Two or three players who are "it" run holding a ball and try to hit the balls being dribbled by the other players with their own ball.
When they score a hit, the two players concerned trade positions.

N.B.:

- **When dribbling in a straight line, the ball can be played with the front end of the foot, the outside of the foot or, at low speed, also with the inside of the foot.**

- **When dribbling with the front end of the foot or outside of the foot, the entire foot should be stretched and pointing towards the ground. When dribbling with the outside of the foot, the foot should also be turned inwards.**

- **When dribbling with the inside of the foot, the foot playing the ball should be pointing slightly upwards and at an angle.**

Variants:

- Which player is the first to dribble through 10 (20) goals without running through the same one twice in succession?
- Two or three "disruptive" players without a ball try to prevent the others from dribbling through the goals by moving the cones.

HOW THE GAME WORKS

Cone course

Cones are used to form five or six goals anywhere in the penalty area. The players each have a ball which they dribble from one of these goals to the next. They can choose their own route, but should dribble the ball through all the goals as quickly as possible. Which player is the quickest at doing this?
When everyone has completed the course, the coach gives the signal to begin again.

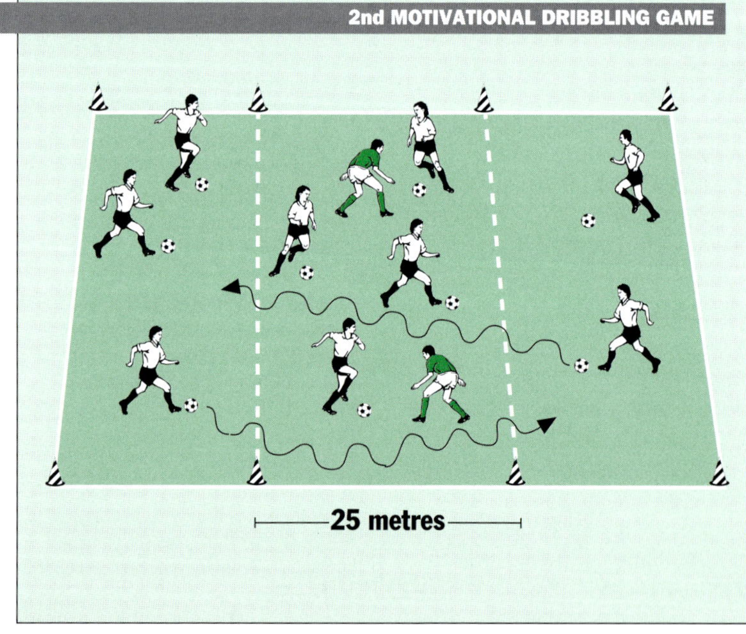

Variant:

- A number of "rocks" (cones, boxes, etc.) are set up as obstacles in an imaginary "river". The players have to dribble around the "rocks" in order to cross the "river". Anyone hitting a "rock" scores a minus point.
- The "river pirates" may only move sideways along a line marked in the middle of the river.

HOW THE GAME WORKS

Crossing the river

Two playing areas approximately 25 metres apart are marked out as "river-bank" zones. Between them is the "river" where between one and three "river pirates", who do not have a ball, "rule". All the other players begin dribbling a ball in one of the two "river-bank" zones. The idea is to "cross the river" as many times as possible in five minutes (i.e. dribbling from one playing area to the other) while being chased by the "river pirates". Anyone losing his ball to a "pirate" immediately trades places with him.

HOW THE GAME WORKS

Obstacle dribbling

The players are divided into two groups of equal size. At first, only the players in one group have a ball each. The players in the other group spread out in the defined playing area and make themselves into obstacles by forming "tunnels" with their feet placed wide apart. The players with a ball try to play through as many "tunnels" as possible in a set time without going through the same "tunnel" twice in succession. Which player can dribble the ball through the most "tunnels" in two minutes?

Variants:

- The players without a ball lie flat on the ground. The players with a ball hop over these obstacles while dribbling.
- The players without a ball make a bridge. The others play the ball under the bridge, jump over it and then continue dribbling at high speed.
- Two players in the "obstacle" group are appointed to be "disruptive", their job being to try and make life more difficult for the players with a ball.

HOW THE GAME WORKS

Target dribbling

The players have a ball each and line up next to each other behind a starting line.
Approximately 15 metres way, between six and 10 markers (cones) are scattered about (one or two fewer than there are players). When instructed, the players take off with their ball and try to reach and thus "capture" one of the cones first.
Those who do not capture a marker score a minus point.
All the players then dribble back to the starting line and wait for the next signal.
Who has the least minus points at the end of the game?

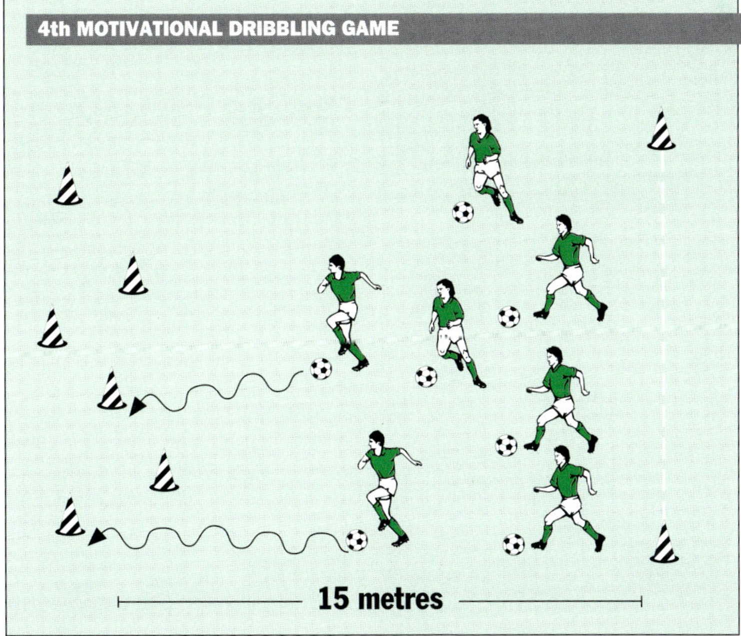

Variants:

- Each cone can be captured by two players.
- The cone has to be knocked over with the ball for it to be "captured".
- The players with a ball have to first get past two or three "disruptive" players moving between the starting line and the cones. Anyone losing his ball becomes a "disruptive" player the next time.

PASSING/ SHOOTING

In this section of training, the players have to be taught the basic technical principles for reliable team-play. This comprises, in particular, the various types of passes.

The best way to ensure precise passing and shooting is to use the inside of the foot, as this provides the largest area of contact with the ball.

Playing with the inside of the foot

Playing with the outside of the foot

Playing with the instep

Hunting "hares"

Two players take hold of each other's hands and move around inside a defined playing area as the "hares". All the other players are "hunters" and have a ball.

The idea is for the "hunters" to shoot at and hit the "hares" as often as possible in one minute. Only hits below hip level count.

A new pair of "hares" is then chosen, and so on.

Which pair of "hares" has been hit the least number of times by the end?

Variants:

■ Same as above, but with two pairs of "hares".

■ Alternative point-scoring system: Which player has scored the most hits at the end of the game?

Medicine ball target

The players have a ball each. The coach (or one of the players) dribbles a medicine ball at random around the pitch. All of a sudden, the coach kicks his ball a bit further ahead, giving a signal at the same time. The players now try to hit the medicine ball as quickly as possible with a precise pass. A point is awarded for each of the first five direct hits. The game then starts again. Which player has accumulated the most points by the end?

Variants:

■ Where larger or weaker groups are involved, two or three players with medicine balls move around the pitch simultaneously.

Cone hunt

Five cones are lined up next to one other along each of the base lines of a defined playing area. Two groups play against each other. Balls are provided for about one third of the players and are distributed equally between the two teams.

The idea is for each group to shoot down all their opponent's cones as quickly as possible. Cones that have been knocked over may not be stood up again. Which is the first team to knock over all the opposing group's cones?

Variants:

■ When a player has knocked over a cone, he holds it up to show the coach and then quickly stands it up again. Which team has shot down the most cones after 10 minutes?

■ A "no-go zone" is marked out in front of the two base lines. The cones must be shot down from outside these zones.

HOW THE GAME WORKS

Cone goal course

The players form pairs and each pair is given a ball. Cones are used to form a number of small goals about 2 metres wide within the playing area.

The idea is for the pairs of players to pass the ball to each other through the small goals as often as possible, changing the goal each time. Which is the first pair to pass to each other through 10 goals?

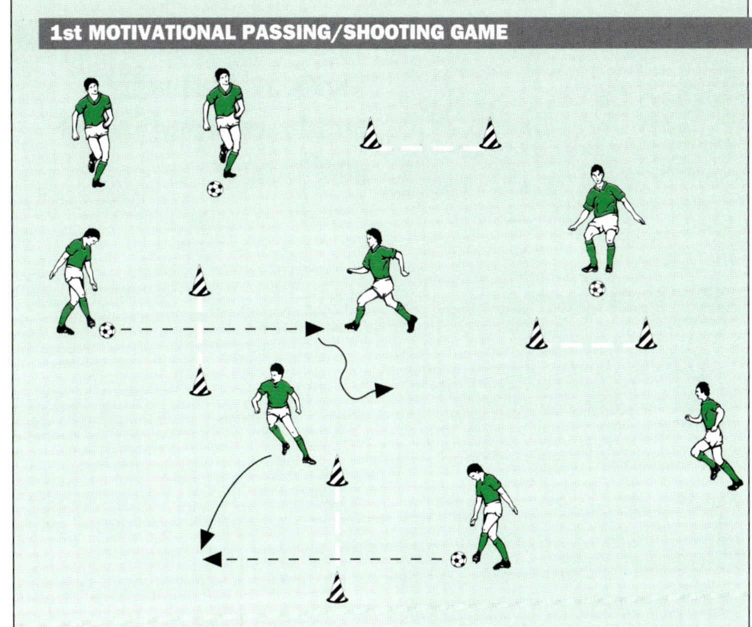

Variants:

- Which pair has made the most passes through the goals after five minutes?
- Between two and four defenders are identified by means of identical sashes, training shirts etc. They then try to make it difficult for the pairs of players to pass to each other – not by tackling the players directly while they are dribbling, but by blocking the way through the goals.

HOW THE GAME WORKS

Passing before shooting

Two goals with goalkeepers are placed 20 to 30 metres apart in such a way that they are not directly opposite each other. A "shooting line" is marked out approximately 8 metres in front of each goal.
Pairs of players line up in front of each goal in roughly equal numbers. The first two pairs then pass the ball to each other while moving forward and take a shot at goal from the "shooting line". After taking their shot, they collect the ball again and line up behind the second group.

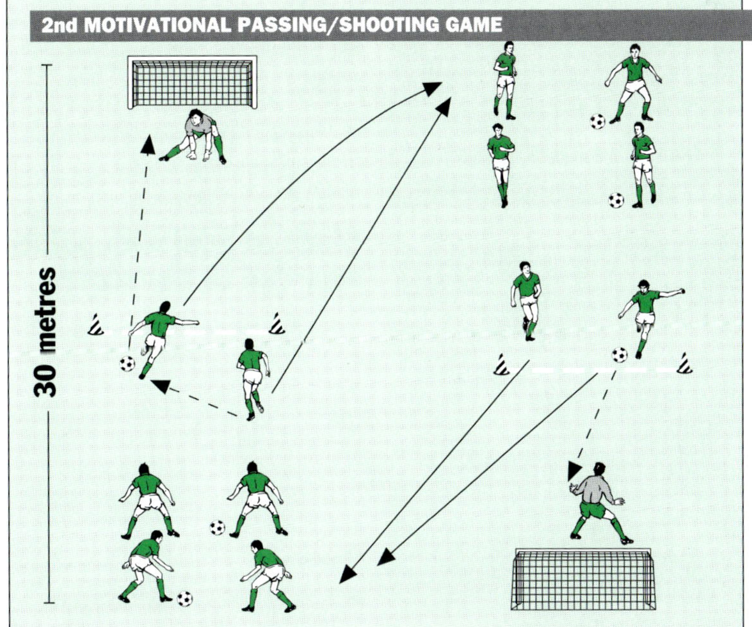

Variant:

- The players are not allowed more than two touches of the ball (1st contact: ball control; 2nd contact: precise pass).

N.B.:

- When kicking with the inside of the foot, the leg taking the weight should be bent slightly at the knee. The ankle of the foot playing the ball should be kept rigid, while the foot itself points to the side and is bent upwards.
- The ball is right next to the leg taking the weight – area of contact between the ball of the foot and the heel.
- The kicking leg follows through the ball.

SHOOTING

Scoring goals is the most enjoyable thing about soccer. So youth players must be given as many opportunities to do this in training as possible. This guarantees a strong sense of achievement.

Back-swing

Shooting with the instep

Follow-through

Shots at goal with points awarded to the goalkeeper

Between three and five players each have a ball and line up behind each other between 7 and 10 metres from a goal guarded by a goalkeeper.

The players take alternate shots at the goal. If a player does not score, he goes to the back of the line. When a goal is scored, the scorer trades places with the goalkeeper. One point is awarded to the goalkeeper for each save (and for each missed shot).

Which player has the most points at the end?

Variants:

- The players take their shot at goal after a short dribble.
- The players kick the ball forward about 5 metres, then run after it and shoot.
- The players first dribble the ball through a slalom course and then shoot.

Shots at goal with points awarded to the scorer

Up to five players each have a ball and line up in front of a goal guarded by a goalkeeper. They place the ball and take shots at goal alternately from approximately 10 metres. Who has scored the most goals after between six and eight attempts?

Variants:

- The distance away from the goal is changed.
- The players are only allowed to shoot with their weaker foot.
- The players shoot after dribbling the ball a short distance.
- The players knock the ball forward and then shoot.

Crossbar shooting competition

Between four and six players each have a ball and line up behind a shooting line about 10 metres from a normal goal. They then try to hit the crossbar.

Who is the first to succeed?

Variants:

- Which player can hit the crossbar the most times in 5 minutes?
- Shooting from the edge of the penalty area: Who can shoot into the empty goal the most times without the ball touching the ground before it crosses the goal line?

Target shooting

Two groups of the same size line up facing each other behind "shooting lines". Skittles and cones are placed next to each other in the centre area between the teams. Each player starts with his own ball. The idea is for the groups to knock over as many targets as possible within a set time through precise shooting. Balls that come to rest in front of the line have to be dribbled back.

Variants:

- Individual competition: each player tries individually to shoot down as many targets as possible.

■ If this game is played indoors, the targets can be stood on a bench in the middle of the playing area. The players then have to knock the cones, etc. off the bench with precise shots, making them land in the opponent's half.
■ A number of small goals are set up on the half-way line of the playing field between the two teams. Which team has scored the most goals after five minutes?

Clear the hurdle

Two groups of between two and four players each stand in one half of a playing area measuring about 10 x 15 metres divided into two parts by an obstacle (benches, hurdles placed next to each other, two 5 x 2 metres goals placed next to each other, a rope stretched across, etc.). One of the groups has a ball.
The idea is for the player in possession to do a drop kick over the obstacle, so that the ball bounces or would bounce in the opponent's half. The opposing team has to catch the ball after the first bounce at the latest and kick it back into the other half.
If the ball hits the obstacle, bounces twice or goes out of play, the opposing team is awarded a point. The first ball of each "rally" has to be played from behind the base line.

Variant:

■ The ball may not bounce in the team's own half but has to be caught on the volley and kicked back.

3-a-side game with individual shots at goal

Two goals are set up about 25 to 30 metres apart. A group of three players lines up by each goal. The players in one group each have a ball.

They then dribble one after another from the goal line to the half-way line and shoot at goal.

One player in the other group acts as goalkeeper while his two team-mates stand behind the goal and act as ball-boys. This avoids long interruptions during the game. When all the players in the first group have taken their shots, the teams switch around.

Which team scores the most goals after five shots per player?

Variants:

■ The players dribble the ball diagonally towards the half-way line and shoot at the end of their angled run.
■ The players knock the ball forward, run onto it and have to shoot before they reach the half-way line.
■ The coach stands on the half-way line. The player with the ball passes to the coach from the goal line and follows it up. The coach then lays on a return pass for the shot at goal.
■ The players first have to dribble through a slalom course before shooting.

Solo run at goal– but one of the real "greats" has other ideas! A dream situation for just about every player...

1st MOTIVATIONAL SHOOTING GAME

Variants:

- The groups shoot alternately at a smaller goal in the middle (no goalkeeper).
- The players dribble the ball a short distance before shooting at goal.
- The goalkeeper rolls the ball to the player, who then moves a few steps with the ball before shooting.
- The goalkeeper throws the ball to the player, who brings it under control and then shoots.

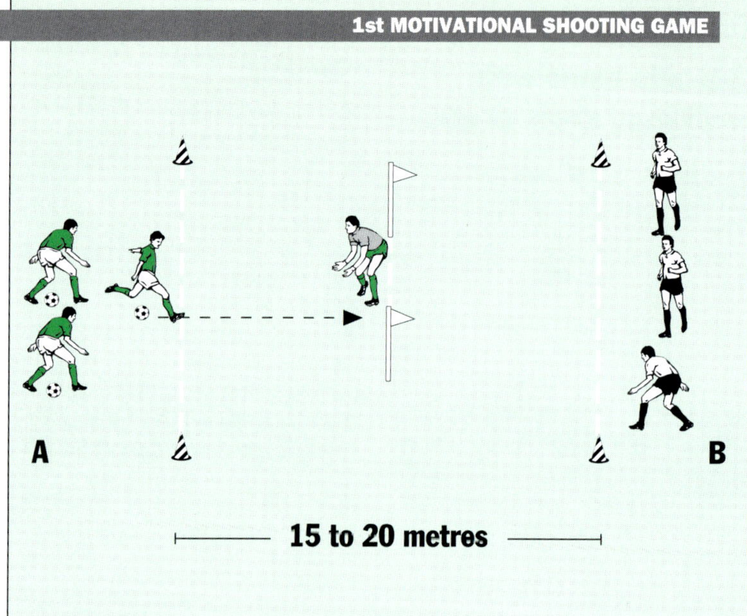

HOW THE GAME WORKS

Shooting at a goal in the middle

Two groups of three to four players stand facing each other about 15 to 20 metres apart (depending on the players' ability). In the middle, poles are used to form a goal about 6 metres wide guarded by a goalkeeper.
The players in one group each have a ball and shoot at the goal, followed by the other group. Which group has scored the most goals after two (three, four) rounds?

2nd MOTIVATIONAL SHOOTING GAME

Variants:

- Any player shooting above knee height has to perform an additional task.
- Individual competition: Which player has shot the ball through the zone the most times after 10 minutes?
- Group competition: The three zones are occupied by three groups of players of equal size. The two outer groups try again to shoot through the goalkeeper zone. The goalkeepers place the balls they catch at the edge of the playing area. The game lasts until all the balls are out of play. Which goalkeeper group is fastest at this?

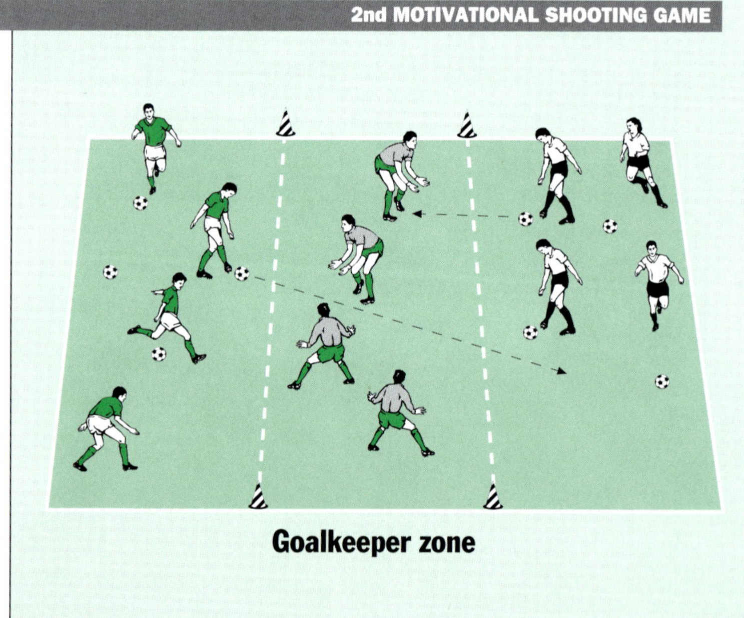

HOW THE GAME WORKS

Shooting through a "goalkeeper zone"

A playing area measuring about 30 x 40 metres is divided into three zones with an equal number of players in each. In the middle is the "goalkeeper zone". Each player in the outer zones has a ball. The idea is for these players to shoot the ball low through the "goalkeeper zone" to the other side as often as possible.
The goalkeepers in the middle zone try to intercept the balls. When a player loses his ball to a goalkeeper, the two players trade positions immediately.

HOW THE GAME WORKS

1-on-1 against 1 shooting game

Groups of three players practice shooting into an approximately 5-metre-wide goal marked out using poles as follows: players A and B stand facing each other on either side of the goal 15 to 20 metres apart. Player C is the goalkeeper. A and B shoot at the goal alternately.
Any player scoring a goal takes over as goalkeeper. The goalkeeper is awarded a point for each save he makes.
Which player has the most points after a set time?

3rd MOTIVATIONAL SHOOTING GAME

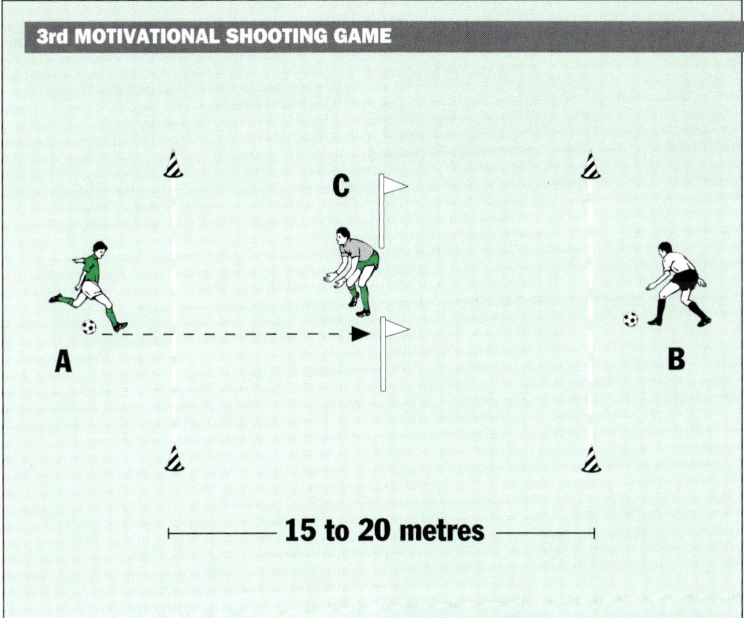

Variants:

- The player can shoot again if the ball rebounds.
- The player drops the ball, lets it bounce once and then shoots.
- The player drops the ball and volleys it with the front end of the foot.
- The player dribbles the ball in a straight line or diagonally towards the goal and shoots in front of a marked line.
- The goalkeeper simply rolls the ball out to the player, who then takes a first-time shot at goal if possible.

HOW THE GAME WORKS

2-a-side against 2 shooting game

Three pairs of players practice together. Two pairs, A and B, stand facing each other 15 to 20 metres apart. In the middle is an approximately 6-metre-wide goal formed using poles which is guarded by pair C. The players in pair A then shoot in succession, followed by those in pair B. Every five minutes, one pair changes places with the goalkeeping pair.
Which pair has scored the most goals after a set time?

4th MOTIVATIONAL SHOOTING GAME

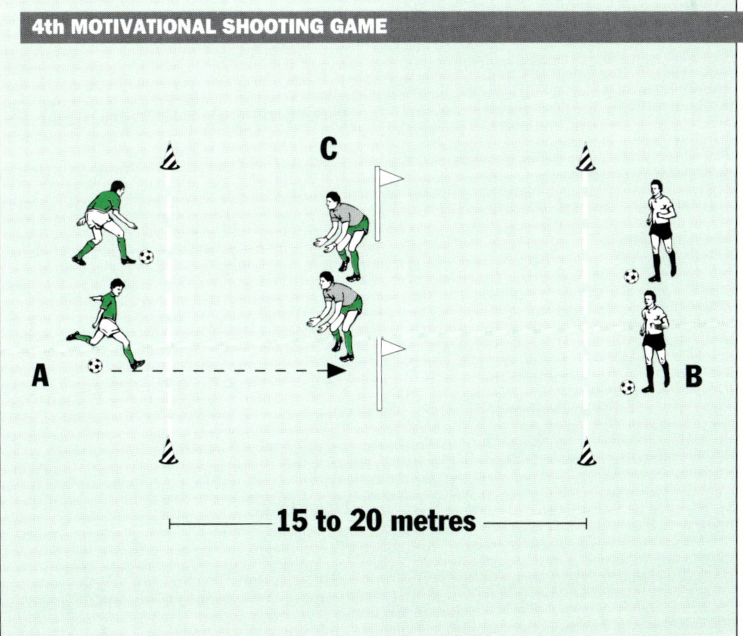

Variants:

- One player uses a short pass to set up his team-mate for a shot.
- One player throws his partner a high ball. The other brings it under control and then shoots.
- The same game with three groups of three players: three players take turns in shooting at the (enlarged) goal from one side. The goal is guarded by the three goalkeepers making up the third group.

HEADING

Playful training focusing on heading can already start with the very youngest players. But remember not to use balls that are too heavy or hard. Why not start off with soft balls?

Jumping

Positioning body and head

Heading with the forehead

Heading a thrown ball I

Five players stand around a roughly 5-metre-wide goal formed using poles. They throw the ball to each other and try to head it into the goal.
Each player takes over as goalkeeper for one minute.
Who lets in the fewest goals?

Variants:

- Goals scored when a team-mate lays on a headed pass for the player heading the goal count double.
- A circle is drawn around the goal, the radius of which is suited to the ability of the players. Either headers are not allowed from within this zone, or goals headed from outside the zone count double.
- The goal is made smaller or enlarged, depending on the ability of the players.

Heading a thrown ball II

Two groups of three players practice in front of a roughly 5-metre-wide goal made from poles. The players in one group are the goalkeepers. The players in the other group throw each other the ball outside a defined zone and try to head the ball into the goal.
After 10 attempts the groups trade places.
Which group heads the most goals?

Variant:

- Only two players stand in the goal. The third player stops the balls behind the goal so as to prevent wasting time.

Handball and heading around a goal

Two groups (of between three and five players) play handball around a roughly 5-metre-wide goal formed using poles and guarded by a goalkeeper.
Goals can be scored from either side, though only with the head and after a pass from a team-mate. If the goalkeeper catches the ball, he then throws it back into the playing area in a neutral way. The ball may not be bounced and a maximum of three steps are allowed with the ball. After a goal, the game resumes immediately.

Heading tag

All the players run around a 15 m x 15 m playing area. Three players who are "it" each carry a ball and chase the other players, trying to hit them by throwing up their ball and heading it at them.
When a player is hit, he trades places, taking his turn to be "it".

HOW THE GAME WORKS

Doubles competition

Two pairs of players occupy an area with a roughly 5-metre-wide goal formed using poles. One player in the first group is the goalkeeper, while the other stands behind the goal and acts as ball-boy. The players of the other group each have a ball.
They take alternate headers from a line approximately 5 metres in front of the goal. Each player throws his own ball in the air and heads at the goal from a standing position. After 10 headers per player, the pairs trade places.

1st MOTIVATIONAL HEADING GAME

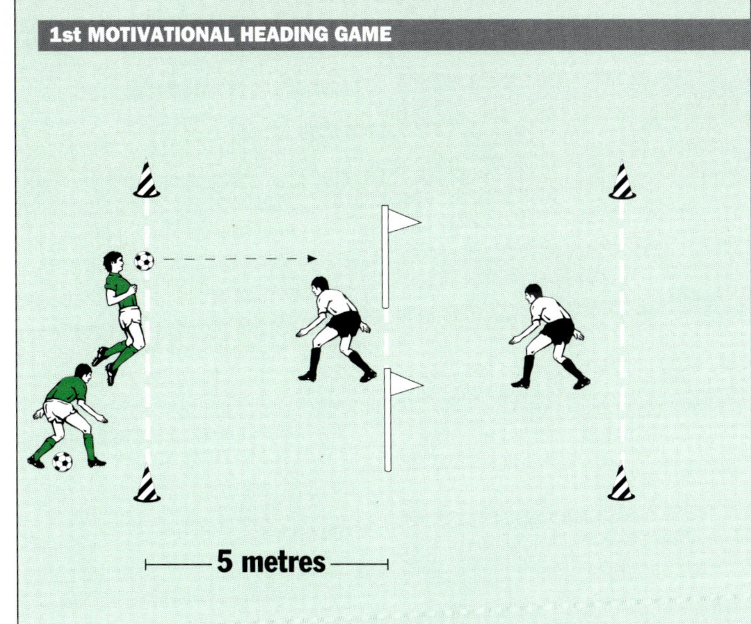

Variants:

- One player throws up the ball for his partner to head. After 10 attempted headers, they switch round.
- Timed competition: which pair has headed the most goals after three to five minutes?
- The pairs start running towards the goal from approximately 20 metres out, with one player throwing the ball up a few times for his partner to head. This player then tries to head the ball back into his partner's hands. At the line, the player heads for goal.

HOW THE GAME WORKS

Individual competition

Two players have a heading competition using two goals formed using poles (approximately 5 metres wide) placed about 6 metres apart.
One player throws up the ball and tries to head it into the other player's goal. The other player can either catch the ball and then head it from his own goal line or try to prevent a goal by attempting a (flying) header. In this case, the player making the save can then head at the opponent's goal from the half-way line.

2nd MOTIVATIONAL HEADING GAME

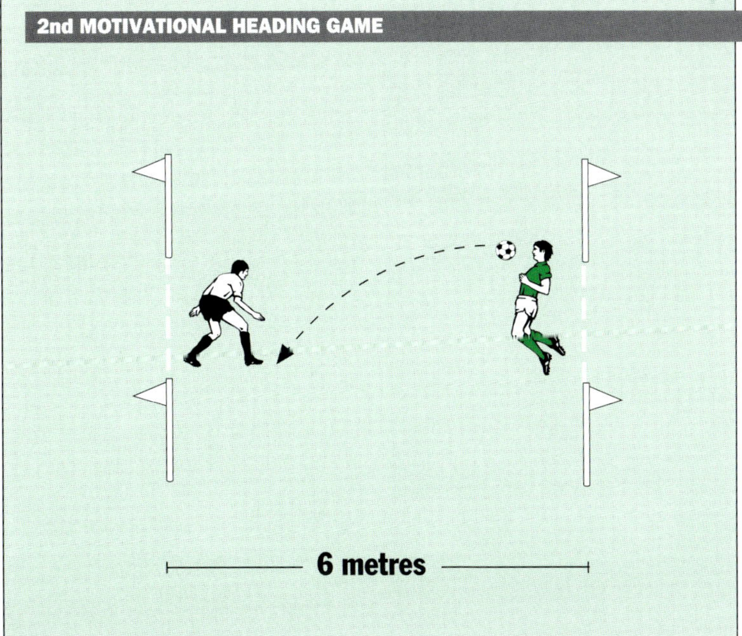

Variants:

- Which player has headed the most goals after five minutes?
- The size of and distance between the goals can be altered.
- The ball is thrown up "fairly" by one player for the other to head.
- The ball is thrown at various heights and from various distances. The player heading the ball must react quickly and move to the ball in such a way as to make the best contact possible.

1-ON-1 SITUATIONS

1-on-1 is a key basic situation in soccer. So players have to learn early on how to make skilful and successful tackles, both in attack and defense.

Controlling the direction of a run

Running alongside

Attacking the ball

1-on-1 around an open goal

Up to four pairs play 1-on-1 simultaneously around a small goal about 2 metres wide formed using cones or poles. The idea is for the player on the ball to get past his marker and score a goal. Goals can be scored from either side. After a goal, the game continues immediately. The players may not run through the goal. Individual games should not last for more than one minute.

Variants:

- The ball has to be dribbled through the goal to score.
- The pairs play 1-on-1 around a makeshift goal (5 metres wide) made up of poles guarded by a goalkeeper.
- After each run-through and a short break, new pairs are formed within the group for the next 1-on-1 game. Which player has scored the most goals at the end?
- One pair of players are goalkeepers in a larger goal. The other pairs again play 1-on-1 around the goal. After each run-through and a short break, another pair takes over as goalkeepers.
- Indoor version: the pairs play around a small box/bench/medicine ball. The attackers have to hit these targets from a 1-on-1 play situation.
- Only one pair at a time plays 1-on-1 around a small goal.

1-on-1 into two small goals

Two or three pairs of players play 1-on-1 simultaneously into two small goals formed using cones or poles and placed about 15 metres apart.
Each player defends one goal. When a player wins the ball, he switches to attacking the other goal. The game should not last more than 30 seconds and should be followed by a short break.

Variants:

- The players can score from either side of the opponent's goal.
- After each round, new pairs are formed within the group for the next 1-on-1 game.
Which player scores the most goals?
- Only one pair plays 1-on-1 between two small goals.
- Playing across lines: to score, the player in possession has to dribble the ball through his opponent's goal.
- The small goals are set up at random on the pitch. The player on the ball has to dribble through one of the goals to score. After scoring, he retains possession of the ball and can attack another goal immediately.

CIRCUIT TRAINING

1-on-1 in defense and attack

The group is divided into pairs of more or less equal ability for circuit training. These pairs run around a circuit in which 1-on-1 games alternate with technical exercises for active relaxation.
Time per individual exercise: two minutes

SUGGESTIONS FOR INDIVIDUAL EXERCISES

Exercise 1:
1-on-1 into two small makeshift goals made up of cones

Exercise 2:
Target shooting into a small goal (2 metres wide) from about 8 to 10 metres

Exercise 3:
1-on-1 around a goal 4 metres wide: to score, the attacker has to dribble the ball across the goal line

Exercise 4:
Target shooting at the crossbar from approximately 10 metres out

Exercise 5:
1-on-1 into two goals (5 metres wide) guarded by goalkeepers

Exercise 6:
Free ball play

Exercise 7:
1-on-1 between two base lines whereby the attacker has to dribble the ball across the opponent's base line

Exercise 8:
Dribbling through a slalom course

HOW THE GAME WORKS

1-on-1 games into three small goals

Three small goals are set up next to each other on each base line of a playing area measuring 40 x 20 metres. Each group consists of six players.
Three players from each group alternate in playing 1-on-1. Each of the players taking a break stands behind one of their goals. The three pairs on the pitch play simultaneously. The players in possession of the ball can score in any of the opponent's goals.
The players within the groups trade places after one minute.

1st MOTIVATIONAL 1-ON-1 GAME

Variants:

- The goals are widened to 5 metres. The players taking a break act as goalkeepers.
- To score, the player must dribble the ball across the opponent's goal line.
- Each pair plays 1-on-1 into two goals facing each other.

N.B.:

- The defender should move around constantly between the goal and the attacker. He must not tackle his opponent too hastily but rather wait patiently for the ideal moment to win possession of the ball.

HOW THE GAME WORKS

1-on-1 into 2 goals with goalkeepers

Two goals 5 metres wide are set up opposite each other about 15 metres apart and guarded by goalkeepers. Two pairs of players play 1-on-1 simultaneously. Each player defends one goal together with his goalkeeper and attacks the other.
The game should not last longer than one minute.
Where applicable, easy exercises can be set for active relaxation between the individual games.

2nd MOTIVATIONAL 1-ON-1 GAME

Variants:

- Only one pair at a time plays 1-on-1 into two goals guarded by goalkeepers.
- The goalkeepers trade places with the other players from time to time – three pairs playing simultaneously on each pitch.

N.B.:

- At the right moment, the attacker has to break through by selling a dummy or outplaying his opponent and then shoot.

DIVIDING UP THE TRAINING AREA

Attractive and effective youth training is organized in small groups. One half of the pitch can be divided up into many different kinds of small playing areas. Excessively large playing areas are too demanding on the youngest players, favour juniors who are good runners but weak players, and hinder optimum learning progress in playing terms. The standard pitches presented here show how easily various game combinations can be organized in different areas at the same time (circuit training, tournament format).

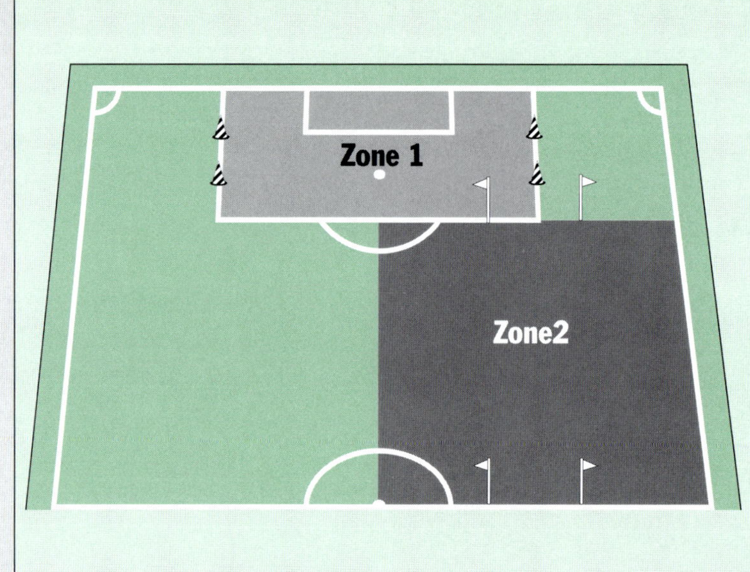

Zone 1 (penalty area):

■ Passing exercises during the warm-up programme

■ Shooting games played into one goal (e.g. 3-a-side) with the line marking the edge of the penalty area acting as a "counter-line"

■ 3-a-side/4-a-side

Zone 2 (35 x 40 metres):

■ Games to finish off with (5-a-side/6-a-side)

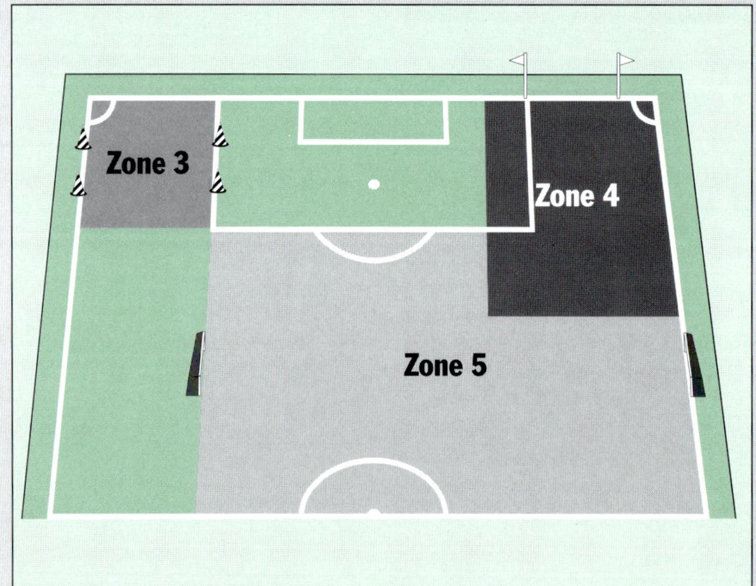

Zone 3 (15 x 15 metres):

■ Tag and running games
■ 1-on-1/2-a-side into small goals
■ Ball games played in small groups (e.g. "piggy in the middle")
■ Dribbling exercises during the warm-up programme

Zone 4 (20 x 30 metres):

■ 4-a-side into goals/across lines

Zone 5 (35 x 55 metres):

■ Official 7-a-side competitive games

CHAPTER 3

Intermediate training

MORE TEACHING MATERIAL FOR TRAINING AND MOTIVATING YOUNG PLAYERS

New ideas

Soccer Training – especially in the development phase – should not only be achievement oriented, but also be motivating, medically responsible, methodically structured and creative. For a coach, the trick is to constantly stimulate players and come up with new ideas.

In the magazine SUCCESS IN SOCCER, experienced soccer experts from the U.S. and Germany will give you – in six issues a year – lots of practical answers to the following questions:

Questions

- How do I teach technical skill in a performance and a age appropriate way?
- How do I teach my team basic tactics or a specific system?
- How should fitness training with the ball be structured?
- What do I have to consider, when planning my training session and shedule?
- What kind of games will keep my training sessions light and interesting?

Besides articles covering soccer techniques, tactics and methods, you will find helpful tips for constructing development and training plans, as well as how to manage your team. SUCCESS IN SOCCER will inform you of the latest development in teaching methods, sports medecine and sports psychology.

More information

You can receive more information about SUCCESS IN SOCCER through Manni Klar, P.O. Box 92046, Albuquerque NM 87199, Phone: 888-828-4263, Fax: 505-232-3162 (for North and South America) or Philippka-Verlag, P.O. Box 6540, D-48034 Münster, Phone +49-251-230050, Fax +49-251-2300599 (other continents.)

Building up players' performance

As a rule the second stage of training is directed at the D and C junior age groups (up to 14 years of age).
This package is broken down to keep pace with the biological development of girls and boys before puberty (D juniors) and during the first phase of puberty (C juniors).

The main task in this age group is to build up individual players' performance and provide juniors with a solid technical and tactical basis.
The specific objectives of the second stage of training include:

- Systematic improvement and consolidation of various sequences of movement (technique)
- Learning and improving individual and team tactical moves
- Acquisition of further specific theoretical knowledge
- Improvement of basic footballing fitness (agility, dexterity, stamina, strength and speed)
- Introduction to specific positional functions in the 11-a-side game
- Encouraging players' willingness to perform and compete
- Teaching teamwork and fair play.

D junior level

Youngsters in this age group (up to 12 years of age) display the following character traits: self-confidence, enjoyment of physical activity, a thirst for knowledge and a willingness to learn and perform. Their physical size is also well-matched by muscular development. In addition, D juniors have a good sense of coordination. This balance between their physical and psychological states is why the D junior phase is regarded as the "golden age of learning."
Building on the basic sports training provided at the F and E junior levels, systematic training specifically geared to soccer can now commence.

C junior level

From the ages of 12 to 13 onwards, drastic physical and psychological changes start to take place, the most noticeable indications of this being the advent of sexual maturity and accelerated growth.
Accordingly, individuals' sense of coordination wanes and they become prone to frequent mood swings. However, this does not necessarily mean that this stage of development should be regarded as a "time of crisis" or an age to "go easy" on youngsters. Indeed, these aspects of growing up raise new, positive mental and physical possibilities which, with the right training, can form a solid basis for further enhancing their performance.

Training for shooting has to be done in small groups to be effective.

OVERVIEW OF D JUNIORS

TRAINING

Boys and girls of this age ...

■ are keen to learn, feel a need to be active and are eager players and achievers.

■ have an excellent sense of co-ordination. Quick, agile movements come relatively easy to them.

■ want to achieve something and have demands made on them.

■ are better equipped mentally, as their powers of concentration improve.

CONSEQUENCES

■ When teaching youngsters what soccer is all about and consolidating this knowledge full advantage must be taken of the basic qualities developed during this "golden age of learning".

■ Making up later for a lack of appropriate training during this phase is extremely difficult and time-consuming.

■ Providing individual players with a solid technique takes priority over their team performance.

■ Playing and practising in small groups is a top priority.

PLAYING

Boys and girls at this age ...

■ love competing. They want to beat others and be better than the rest.
Through their successes, children seek the respect and recognition of their friends, thus developing self-confidence.

■ enjoy playing competitive games against other sides, the high points of club football.

■ can already take in demanding tactical principles and tasks associated with their position.

CONSEQUENCES

■ Of course players and coaches want to win. However, the outcome of the game is less important than the sporting development of the individual junior players.

■ The players must not be put under pressure to succeed. The obsessive ambitions of coaches, parents and clubs have no place in junior soccer.

■ Other taboos include overly narrow tactical assignments, which curb individual players' willingness to take risks, limit their creativity and stifle their personal development.

CARE

Boys and girls at this age ...

■ gradually distance themselves from adults and form closer relationships with their peers.

■ strive to gain recognition from their peers. Individuals' status, and hence their self-confidence, is determined principally by their physical/sporting performance.

■ develop a marked thirst for knowledge.

CONSEQUENCES

■ Training must be made as varied and competitive as possible so that juniors can assess their abilities relative to their fellow players. This gives every player an opportunity to present his own individual strengths and figure amongst the best.

■ Even "annoying" questions asked by young players must be taken seriously and answered patiently.

OVERVIEW OF C JUNIORS

TRAINING

Boys and girls at this age ...

■ "shoot up" in height when they enter puberty. This rapid growth creates an imbalance between the length of their torso and legs.

■ often find it difficult to move around in a fluid manner because of the physical changes they are experiencing.

■ on the other hand demonstrate greatly improved strength and speed.

CONSEQUENCES

■ The basic technical principles already learnt need to be adapted to this greater swiftness.

■ Their enhanced ability to grasp concepts means that they can be taught more demanding tactics.

■ Fitness and stamina are improved, primarily through playing. Training should occasionally be supplemented by simple circuits, jumping exercises, games designed to test their reactions and exercises designed to boost their acceleration.

■ Training must focus regularly on improving players' agility.

PLAYING

Boys and girls at this age ...

■ playing in a competitive team, i.e. in a group which shares the same objectives, norms and interests, find the "security" which they lack or consciously reject in other areas of their lives at this time. Psychological insecurity is stabilized merely by belonging to a team.

■ can also perform more specific tasks within the team because they have a better grasp of the game.

CONSEQUENCES

■ The recognition by team-mates and coaches of the importance of individuals' performance in the team's success helps to boost young players' self-confidence and stimulate the development of their personality. Each player must be given tasks geared towards his particular strengths.

■ However, these specific tasks must on no account stifle or even limit individual initiative, creativity and enjoyment of the game.

■ The main emphasis during games can be placed on the use of space and the careful build-up of play.

CARE

Boys and girls at this age ...

■ distance themselves further from adults, looking to establish their own fixed place in the world.

■ are often prone to considerable mood swings and inconsistency in their performance during this orientation phase.

■ receive support from their friends and peers during this somewhat insecure process of "finding themselves".

CONSEQUENCES

■ Junior players at this age must be shown how to be independent and share responsibility.

■ However, coaches must not issue all the orders, plan and organize everything, block out criticism and avoid or "resolve" conflicts in an authoritarian manner. Instead, their main job is to encourage the youngsters to find their own solutions and develop their own ideas.

■ Each player must be allocated suitable responsibilities.

A sensible combination of playing and training

After learning the basic soccer techniques during the first stage of training, the main objective now is for the junior players to learn and build on the different elements they have learnt, striving for perfection as far as possible.
This means correcting serious mistakes, perfecting sequences of movements in training and then deliberately applying them in specific situations.
The systematic practising of sequences of movements is a process involving dogged repetition. Only through constant practice can defective technique be rectified.
In addition, the exercises set for players must be so varied that at the same time they learn how to apply the right technique in constantly changing game situations.

More difficult techniques, like controlling the ball after a high pass, are trained from the D junior level onwards.

Training on technique must also be combined with real game situations (moves taken from the 11-a-side game). The best way of combining technical and tactical training is to use the many different games played in small teams.
In contrast to basic training, the games played between small teams at the intermediate training stage no longer take place in as carefree a manner as possible. At this stage coaches focus on individual technical and tactical elements by introducing specific additional tasks. To solve these tasks, players have to focus on applying a certain technique in the respective game situation.
The best basic form of the game for doing this is the 4-a-side formation, with the spotlight deliberately directed at individual elements of the game and the many possibilities this format entails. This training is organized in such a way that the young players alternate constantly between playing in a team and performing various exercises concentrating on a particular aspect of their game.

Training focused on specific elements

At this stage, junior coaches should systematically provide training for one element of technique after another. When planning the training programme, the focus must be placed on specific elements which are then worked on until (most of) the players have understood them.
Coaches must then figure out the best types of games and exercises for practising these points and decide how to plan and implement their inclusion in the various training sessions.

Coaches should also tell their players in advance what the objectives of the training session are, making sure that everyone under-

TIPS

Correct sequence for playing and training in practice

1st STEP
The coach sets a task.

2nd STEP
The players try to perform it, look for solutions and thereby gain experience.

3rd STEP
The coach observes the players' movements and assesses how they are fulfilling the task.

4th STEP
The coach discusses his observations with the players. He can either ask the players to come with alternative solutions, demonstrate correct solutions himself or get the players to demonstrate them and then proceed to give them tips on correct movements or actions. The coach can also juxtapose right and wrong solutions or movements.

5th STEP
The players try it out again, gaining experience with the best possible solution.

WEEKLY TRAINING

TRAINING SESSION 1	TRAINING SESSION 2	COMPETITIVE GAME
▶ Practising ball skills ▶ Running and relay games ▶ Playful gymnastics ▶ Games played in small teams (4-a-side) focusing on particular technical and tactical aspects ▶ In between, exercises to practice the same technical/ tactical element ▶ Finish off with games played in small teams trying to score goals against each other	▶ Practising ball skills/exercises in agility ▶ Playful gymnastics ▶ Games focusing on a particular technical/tactical aspect (e.g. repeating and building on the main emphasis of the first training unit) ▶ In between, exercises to practice the same technical/ tactical element ▶ Finish off with a 7-a-side (or 6-a-side) game, with the teams (including goalkeepers) trying to score goals against each other	▶ The objective of the 2nd stage of training is to play 11-a-side on a standard pitch (measuring approx. 105 x 70 metres) ▶ Transition from a small pitch to a standard pitch (gradual) ▶ Systematic teaching of basics for playing on a standard pitch: – Use of space/positional play – Positional groups – Tasks of the various positions – Tasks within positional groups

stands them. This will help to consciously involve the players in the learning process. Experience shows that this speeds up the learning process.

Tips on weekly planning and the training units

▶ It is important to focus on particular points at specific stages of training and then concentrate on these. This means presenting the players with challenges in real learning situations.

▶ The duration of these stages of training will depend on the progress made by the players.

▶ If the players are to remember what they are taught in the long term, their training should focus on individual technical/tactical elements over continuous periods lasting at least 3 to 4 training units, depending on the level of difficulty and priority assigned to the element in question. Remember, children need time to familiarize themselves with tasks in games played in small teams and in exercises. Experience shows that players are not normally given enough time to practise individual basic elements of the game for them to achieve visible successes.

▶ Games and exercises must be repeated regularly both during a training unit and throughout the season.

▶ All training tasks should be set in such a way that they do not appear to be too difficult or too easy for the players (establishment of equal-ability groups to avoid players being overstretched or understretched).

▶ By the D junior level at the latest (introduction of competitive 11-a-side games on a standard pitch), each junior player must be given a chance to play in as many different positions as possible. Only in this way will it become clear where he can best perform in the long term - both personally and on behalf of his team. Moreover, *all-round* training is bound to come in useful later on.

Practical training tips

Tip 1:
Begin each training session with a short pep talk.

The coach calls the players together, welcomes them and tells them briefly about the objectives and content of the day's training.

The following basic principles should be observed:

- The players should either stand or sit in a semicircle in front of the coach. In this way, he can see all the youngsters better and they can follow his instructions/demonstrations more easily.
- The coach only starts talking when everybody has come together and all distractions have been eliminated. Balls should definitely be kept out of reach!
- The coach must not speak too fast. And remember, too much information merely causes confusion, because children and youngsters have short attention spans. So the coach must make his explanations short and to the point, while at the same time radiating "warmth" and empathy. Aloof strictness, showing off and arrogance also have no place in junior soccer.

Tip 2:
Give frequent demonstrations and give clear instructions.

Junior players become confused if they are given too many explanations. On the other hand, if they are shown something they will understand and absorb it more easily and faster. So demonstrations can save a great deal of time and prove more successful than any number of words.

Accordingly, coaches must have the technical and playing ability to perform such demonstrations correctly enough to make them effective.

Tackling practice is also an essential component of training at the D junior level. Simple tactical basics such as shielding the ball with one's body need to be trained at this stage.

Tip 3:
Provide "motivating games" at the start of training.

It is not only small children who like running and jumping about, playing with a ball and giving free rein to their love of movement. D and C juniors also want to run at full pelt and let off steam, especially when they have spent a long time at school and doing homework. For this reason, long-winded explanations and instructions should be avoided at all costs at the beginning of training sessions. Instead, coaches should organize an interesting, easily understandable motivating game which gets going as fast as possible and allows the kids to get everything else out of their system. Another possibility at the start is to give each youngster about five minutes to play with a ball by themselves, offering them a chance to try out informally all the tricks and moves they have learnt so far. This can then be followed by the more demanding aspects of the training session.

Tip 4:
Join in the fun.

Coaches can join in some of the motivating, running and tag games, thereby giving the youngsters a chance to see their coach's own sporting enthusiasm at first hand. Care must be taken, however, to keep a constant eye on all the players as far as possible, so that they can be offered assistance and corrective advice whenever necessary. To this end, participating coaches should select a spot from which they can see all the groups of players at once.

Tip 5:
Keep the organization simple.

Countless training sessions which were perfectly planned in advance have foundered in practice as a result of organizational problems. Since not all such problems can be anticipated, the ability to improvise is an important "virtue" of any decent coach.

Nonetheless, many difficulties can be ruled out from the start by observing a few basic principles:

■ Keep the time required to organize a training session to a minimum so as to avoid confusion (on the part of both the coach and the players).

■ It is a big help if the same organizational aspects (size and composition of groups, pitches, equipment) can be carried over from one training phase to the next. This prevents time being spent on setting things up and prolongs the effective training time.

■ Although the setting up and clearing away of the equipment and pitches is organized by the coach, the physical work should be done by the players themselves. This provides relief for the coach and teaches the children and youngsters how to work together as a team.

■ As far as possible, all preparations for training should be completed before the start of the session, thereby ensuring that everything goes off smoothly. This includes putting out balls, cones, training shirts, markers, setting up goals, etc.

Tip 6:
Finish each training session with a short discussion.

■ When training is over, the players should come together, as they did at the start, and be offered a chance to say what they thought of the session - i.e. asked what was "great", "boring" or "too difficult", or "what should we do again?"

■ If a competitive match is to be played at the weekend, the players must be informed of the meeting place and told the kick-off time. It might be possible to organize the journey for an away game with the help of the players' parents.

■ Finally, the coaches should check the changing-rooms to make sure that the youngsters have left nothing behind.

ORGANIZING TRAINING

TRAINING GROUND:

Which training ground is available? Will other teams be there at the same time? Do any arrangements have to be made?
What condition is the ground in? Does this rule out certain exercises or games? How should the available space be divided up to enable the youngsters to play and practice with the fewest disruptions?

TRAINING MATERIAL:

Which training material is available? Are there enough balls for everyone to practise individual skills if need be? If not, how can the training session be organized to give each player as much contact with the ball as possible? What can I use as markers to clearly define the boundaries of the pitches for the small-team soccer games? How can I set up the training equipment and markers in such a way that switching from one exercise to the next does not require complex and time-consuming reorganization?

SIZE OF TRAINING GROUP:

How many players are in the training session? How many groups and pitches must I make in order to intensify the learning process of playing in small teams? What can I do if the size or ability of the teams varies too greatly?

COMPETITIVE 7-A-SIDE AND 11-A-SIDE GAMES

Competitive games during training

Competitive games fulfil a valuable function at all levels of training – as long as they are adapted to the ability and interests of the respective age group.

Children learn primarily during and through playing. They enjoy competing with youngsters their own age and showing their parents, brothers and sisters, and friends what they are capable of. They proudly display what they have learnt while, at the same time, looking for recognition of their performance.

This positive and open attitude towards competitive games can, however, turn into frustration if

– the individual is not involved much in the game,

– it results in feelings of failure,

– players do not get a chance to perform.

The team's performance should never be assessed solely on the basis of the outcome of the game. Whether it wins or loses, the coach must encourage individual players, point out where progress has been made, give praise where praise is due and always be friendly.

Pitch and basic formation for competitive 7-a-side games

NB:

Advantages of the 7-a-side game

- **This is ideal as a competitive game for children up to the age of 10 when played in an area between the penalty area and half-way line.**
- **This form of competitive game provides maximum enjoyment and excitement and optimal learning opportunities for both beginners and young talents.**
- **This is because juniors can follow the game easily and even the less-talented players are repeatedly in the thick of the action.**

From small-pitch soccer to the 11-a-side game

The 7-a-side game played on a reduced-size pitch is the official competitive game for all F and E junior teams.

Only D juniors and upwards are capable of switching to the "big time" and playing regular, competitive 11-a-side matches. However, it should also be possible to continue with 7-a-side matches played on a small pitch as the official competitive game for juniors at this level, especially where weaker teams are concerned, or clubs lacking juniors in this age group. There must be flexibility in organizing games.

Guidelines for competitive 11-a-side football

Not only team and pitch size have to be adapted to the level of ability of the players concerned. Game concepts, basic formations, responsibilities and demands made on the players in various positions also vary with the age group concerned, competitive experience, etc. Systems of play and tactics must neither understretch or overtax junior players. Even if it is tempting to do so, junior team coaches must under no circumstances attempt to impose the trends appearing in, say, professional soccer on their children's or junior teams.

Sharing of tasks associated with particular positions and basic formation at this age

Youngsters are introduced systematically to the tasks associated with individual positions in the 11-a-side game during the second phase of their training, after being gradually prepared for it as children in 7-a-side games. It makes sense to spread the 10 outfield players evenly over the pitch.

A distinction is drawn between three areas of action:

- The attacking zone (the domain of strikers)
- The build-up play zone (the domain of midfield players)
- The defensive zone (the domain of defenders and the goalkeeper).

Pitch and basic formation for competitive 11-a-side games

Playing positions:

① Goalkeeper
② Right back
③ Left back
④ Centre back
⑤ Sweeper or second centre back
⑥ Right midfield player
⑦ Outside right
⑧ Left midfield player
⑨ Centre forward
⑩ Central midfield player
⑪ Outside left

At this age, it is quite reasonable to have three attackers (two wingers and a centre forward). The midfield is also best covered by three players (i.e. one on the right, one on the left and one in the centre), who must be capable of switching between offense and defense. It makes sense to have four players in defense, namely two full backs and two centre backs.

Advantages of this basic formation

- The positions in the attacking zone are covered across the full width of the pitch. The ball can be played down the wings or through the middle without making the midfield players do too much running about.
- The midfield players have several passing options when in forward positions.
- Specific build-up play begins in the defensive zone; via the midfield players the ball can be played across the pitch or deep to the strikers.
- The full back positions are filled, thereby enabling the defence to counter attacks launched down the wings by the opposition.

COACHES' MATCH RESPONSIBILITIES

AFTER THE LAST TRAINING SESSION BEFORE A GAME

- **Decide on a time and place to meet, making sure that all the players have understood. Punctuality (on the part of the coach too, in particular) is absolutely essential.**
- **Clarify the exact details of transport to away matches.**
- **Make sure that the kit and equipment is complete. Players must bring their own clean football boots, shinguards, towels, etc.**
- **Make sure that suitable drinks are available.**
- **Giving a short team talk before the game (5 to 10 minutes long), providing some basic information about the match ahead and announcing the team line-up is quite adequate for the younger age groups. Encourage them, fire their enthusiasm.**
- **Allow for a sufficient warm-up so as to arouse their enjoyment of the game.**
- **Fill in the game report sheet or have it filled in by the players' parents.**

DURING THE GAME

- **Encourage the players, spur them on and respond positively. Avoid shouting anything negative (and prevent parents from doing so).**
- **Follow the game closely, in a concentrated fashion so that you can offer assistance, make changes or substitute players whenever necessary.**
- **Give all the substitutes a chance to play if possible.**

AT HALF-TIME

- **Provide the players with drinks. Ask about and treat any injuries.**
- **Don't say too much, just make incisive observations. Address the players individually.**
- **Give them some specific help and tips for the second half. Do not reproach individual players. Motivate the team for its second half performance.**
- **Give the team some final encouragement before sending them back out onto the pitch.**

AFTER THE GAME

- **Praise, console, cheer up or calm down the players. Do not let any arguments break out.**
- **Provide refreshments. Treat any injuries and take care of the arrangements for any further treatment.**
- **Pay attention to hygiene and orderliness, i.e. tell the players to wash and shower, not to leave anything behind and to leave the changing rooms clean.**
- **Say a few words about the next training session.**
- **Sign the game report sheet.**
- **Say goodbye to the opposing team and the referee.**

■ Two centre backs, backing each other up, cover the area most threatened by the opposition's attackers.

Duties when on the attack

■ Players should vary their tactics for attacking, i.e. come from different positions, especially down the wings. For this reason, they have to be fast and good at dribbling, crossing and shooting.
■ The midfield players must be capable of combining well. Their job is to feed the strikers with "intelligent" passes and always be ready to receive the ball. However, when the situation is right, they must also be prepared to take a shot on goal themselves.
■ The defender's job is to pass the ball safely to a midfield player or striker and then make themselves available for further passes.

Defensive duties

■ All players must quickly switch to defense when possession of the ball is lost.
■ The strikers should support the midfield players, and the midfield players should back up the defenders.
■ All players should be allocated a particular area to defend and endeavour to put off or counter any opposing player entering this area.

CONTENTS OF INTERMEDIATE TRAINING

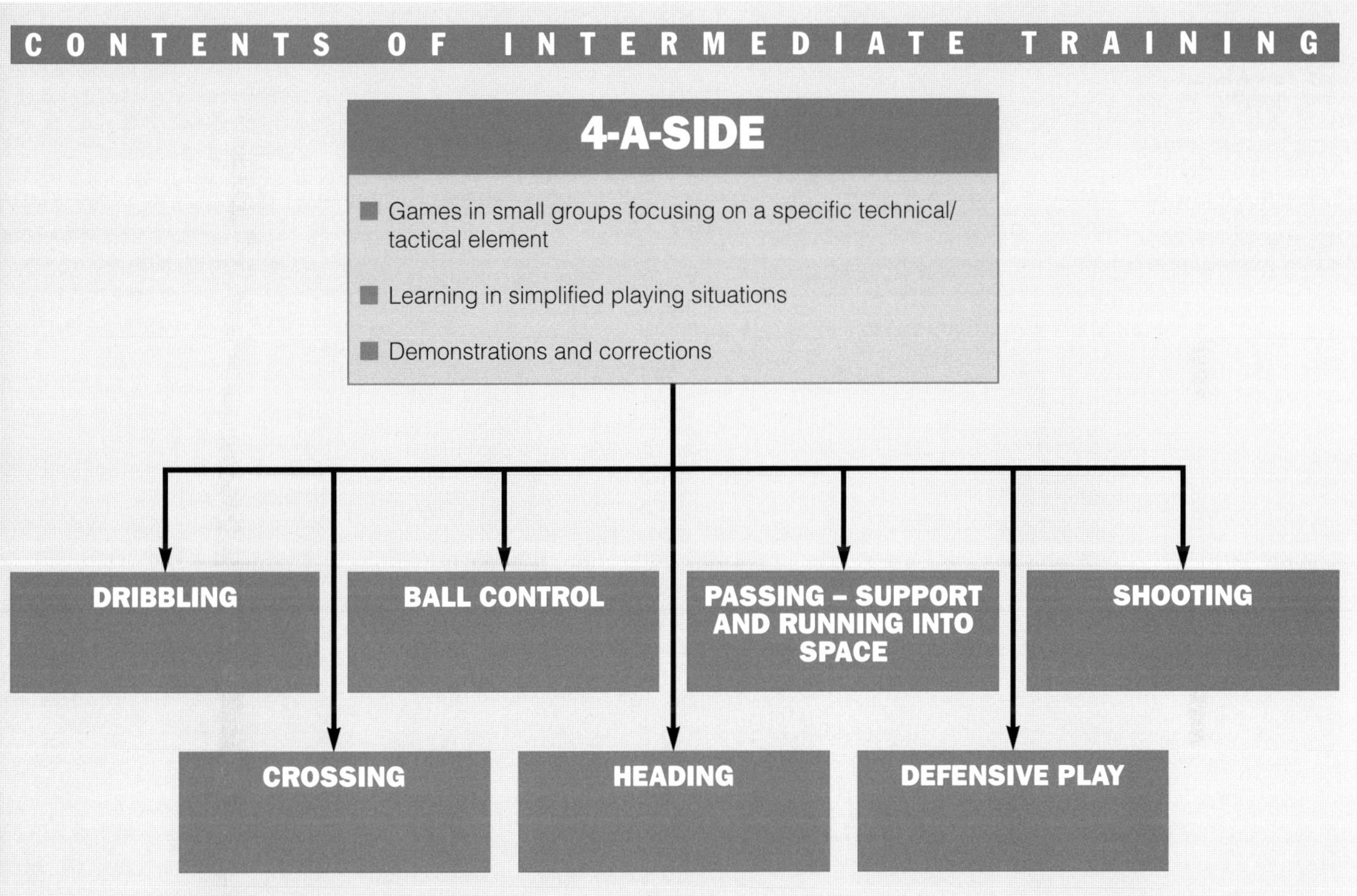

FOOTBALL EXERCISES

- Attractive exercises to supplement the games focusing on particular elements
- Alternate between games and exercises
- Demonstrations and corrections

BALL-SKILL EXERCISES

- Regular warm-up programme content
- Objective: creativity and confidence on the ball
- Ball-skill exercises and feinting movements

ADDITIONAL FITNESS EXERCISES

- Running and jumping competitions
- Games for training agility and coordination
- Soccer games in small groups as the best form of "fitness training"

Ball technique and attractiveness

Everyone wants soccer to be attractive. Nothing fascinates and excites spectators more than a demonstration of the most difficult techniques and spontaneous flashes of brilliance. However, such displays of skill presuppose a high level of technical ability. Every player must stand out through their excellent ball control and creativity when on the ball.

Ball technique and success

However perfectly players master soccer technique, it must never be allowed to become an end in itself.
Above all, optimum ball skills and a perfect playing technique increase the scope for tactical decisions and action on the part of each player and therefore of the team as a whole. Mastery of technique enables teams and individuals to cope in even the most difficult game situations.

It will be even more important in the future to use well-developed and creative ball skills to get out of very tight situations and set up goal-scoring opportunities against strong defensive formations.
In the top flight, matches are decided, above all, by spectacular solo runs and inspired individual moves. Outstanding individualists can become match-winning players if the team as a whole puts on a compact, disciplined and solid performance.

Consequences for basic training on soccer technique

The foundations for near-perfect individual technique have to be laid when the players are still very young.
It is precisely at the E and D junior levels in the so-called "golden age of learning" that young footballers can grasp even very difficult moves easily and quickly when given correct instructions. As a result, specific practice of ball techniques, tricks and feinting manoeuvres in exercises suited to the age group in question makes for rapid progress.
It is all the more important at this stage of training to provide a regular programme of technique-oriented exercises so that the young players can develop into creative, technically competent players whose game is characterized by eagerness and enthusiasm.

Furthermore, the fact that "ball artists" are becoming an increasingly rare breed means that coaches have to display great patience with their youngsters. Comments like "release the ball earlier or you'll be watching the next game from the touch-line" stifle creative, skilful individual moves of the kind that junior players' coaches should be positively encouraging.

TRAINING ON TECHNIQUE

TIP 1: An interesting technical programme comprising a wide variety of ball-based exercises must be included in just about every training unit for this age group.
Such exercises are best suited to the "mood-setting" start of training sessions, though ball training can also take place between individual run-throughs of games, moves or tactics, for example.

TIP 2: The difficulty of the ball exercises must be geared to individual player's degree of ability. Coaches' levels of expectation should only be increased gradually.
Only in this way can the all-important sense of achievement be ensured. The young players will then look forward to the next training session with pleasure and positive expectations.

TIP 3: Coaches must also encourage their youth players to practise a lot with the ball and try out new skills outside their official training programme. For example, a technically difficult exercise can be demonstrated towards the end of the session and the youngsters asked to practice it at home. Volunteers can then be asked to demonstrate the skill in question to the others at the next training session.

TIP 4: Young players learn mainly by copying what they see. For this reason, any skills demonstrated by coaches must be executed perfectly.

TIP 5: Coaches must praise their youngsters when they perform well and be prepared to correct any failings in their technique.

1 Using the inside of the foot

With the players light on their feet, the ball is shifted quickly to and fro between the insides of both feet.

2 Using the inside of the foot on the turn

The ball is shifted to and fro between the insides of both feet while the players turn on the spot.

3 Using the inside of the foot and then rolling the ball

The ball is shifted to and fro between the insides of both feet, then the player rolls the inside of his foot over the ball and carries on dribbling for a few metres. The sequence is then repeated.

4 Ball behind the pivot leg

The ball is dragged back behind the pivot leg using the sole of the free foot and then pushed sideways at an angle of 90 degrees using the inside of the same foot. They then turn slightly towards the ball, etc.

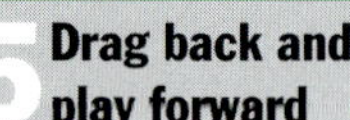

5 Drag back and play forward

The ball is first dragged back using the sole of the foot, then played forward using the inside of the same foot. Finally, the sole of the other foot is placed smartly on the ball, which the player then drags back towards his body.

6 Drag back and dribble forward

The ball is casually dribbled forward, then dragged back a short distance towards the player's body using the sole of the foot. The player pushes the ball forward using his instep and dribbles forward.

7 "Cutting away" using the inside of the foot

A half-turn is now incorporated into the dribbling, using the inside of the foot. Immediately after changing direction, the player accelerates away, still dribbling, for a few metres.

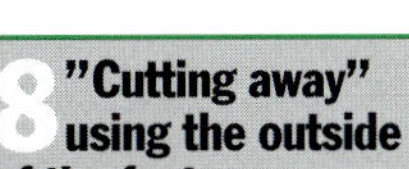

8 "Cutting away" using the outside of the foot

A sudden change of direction is now incorporated into the dribbling, using the outside of the foot. Immediately after changing direction, the player accelerates away, still dribbling, for a few metres.

9 "Cutting away" to the side

The ball is dribbled in a straight line using the outside of the foot. The player then angles his foot, placing the outside of it in front of the ball, before cutting away to the side and accelerating away, still dribbling.

10 Dragging back and to the side (I)

Dribbling the ball, the player drags it back slightly using the sole of his foot before moving the ball sideways a short distance with the inside of the same foot and accelerates away in a different direction, still dribbling.

11 Dragging back and to the side (II)

Same as the above, except that the ball is moved to the side using the outside of the same foot before the player accelerates away, still dribbling.

12 Feigning a shot and then changing direction

Feigning a shot, the player drags the ball behind his body with the sole of the foot and then moves off in the opposite direction, playing the ball with the outside of his other foot.

13 Switching feet with the ball in front of the body (I)

Using the inside of one foot, the player switches the ball to his other foot so that he can start dribbling with the outside of that foot.

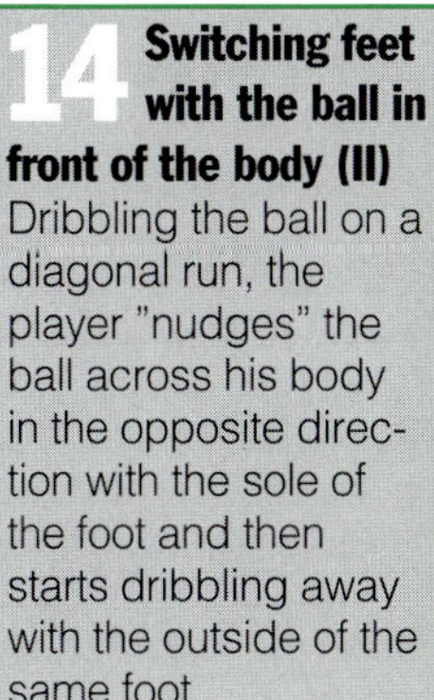

14 Switching feet with the ball in front of the body (II)

Dribbling the ball on a diagonal run, the player "nudges" the ball across his body in the opposite direction with the sole of the foot and then starts dribbling away with the outside of the same foot.

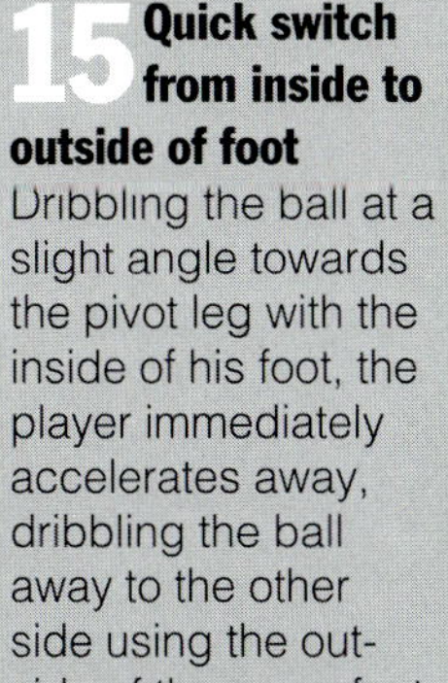

15 Quick switch from inside to outside of foot

Dribbling the ball at a slight angle towards the pivot leg with the inside of his foot, the player immediately accelerates away, dribbling the ball away to the other side using the outside of the same foot.

16 Dragging the ball back behind the pivot leg

While dribbling, the player drags the ball back behind the pivot leg using the sole of the foot and then pushes it forward at 90° to the direction of his run using the inside of the same foot.

17 Stepping over the ball

While dribbling casually, the player steps over the ball with one foot (from the outside to the inside), sets this foot down briefly and then sets off in the other direction, dribbling the ball with the outside of the same foot.

18 "Switch jump" over the ball

The player places the sole of his foot on the ball and jumps past the ball, simultaneously turning around, before setting off in the opposite direction, playing the ball with the outside of the other foot.

19 Changing direction after missing a step

Dribbling the ball on a diagonal run, the player takes a wide step outside behind the ball and then heads off in the other direction, playing the ball with the outside of the other foot..

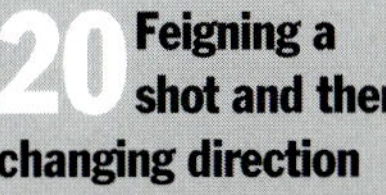

20 Feigning a shot and then changing direction

After making as if to shoot, the player pushes the ball behind his pivot leg with the inside of his free foot and sets off in the opposite direction, playing the ball with the outside of the other foot.

21 "Step-over" (scissors trick)

Dribbling the ball forward, the player steps over the ball to the outside, shifts his weight onto this leg and then dribbles off in the opposite direction, playing the ball with the outside of the other foot.

DRIBBLING

Dribbling is the most important basic technique in the game of soccer. Players must gradually learn to keep the ball under control at all times, i.e. keep it close to their feet. At the same time, they should look up from the ball more often with a view to registering the positions of the other players at all times.

BASIC GAME # 1

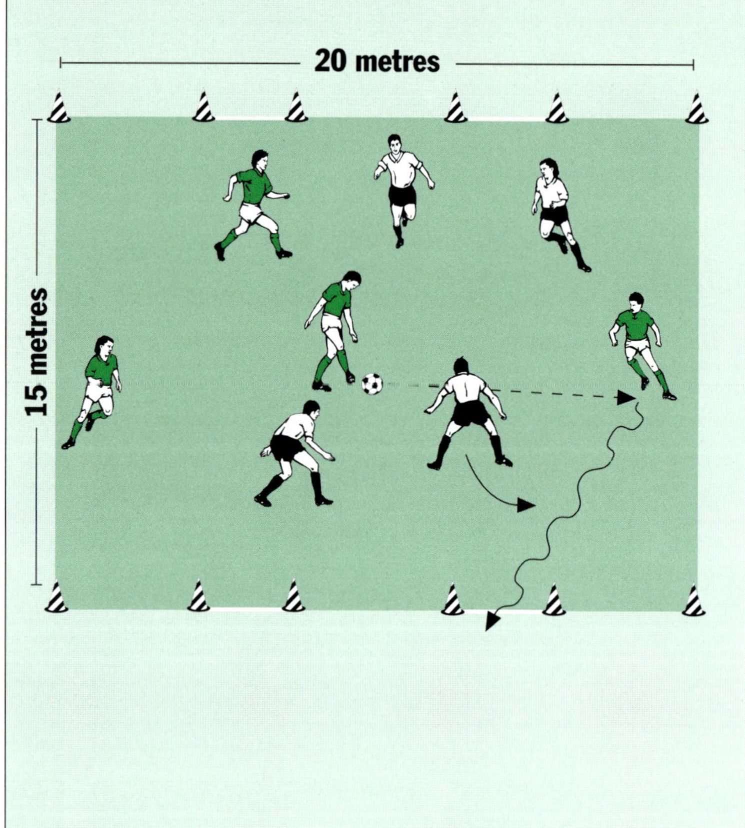

HOW THE GAME WORKS

4-a-side with four small goals

Two makeshift goals (cones, poles, etc.) are set up on the goal lines of a pitch measuring 20 x 15 metres. To score, the ball has to be dribbled through one of the small goals from 4-a-side play. After a goal the team which scored remains in possession of the ball. To continue the game, the goal-scorer may dribble the ball onto the pitch or pass it to a team-mate from any point off the pitch.
The ball has to be dribbled through a different goal to score again.
The defending players may only challenge the player in possession of the ball when he is on the pitch.

Duration of the game: 5 minutes

Variant 1:
Three goals are set up on each goal line.
To score, the ball has to be dribbled through one of the goals.

Variant 2:
After a goal has been scored, the team conceding it is given possession of the ball. To continue the game, one of its players may dribble the ball onto the pitch or pass to a team-mate from any point off the pitch.

Variant 3:
4-a-side from goal line to goal line. The players have to dribble the ball through one of the two goals on the *opposite* goal line to score.
The team scoring a goal remains in possession of the ball.

CORRECTIVE HELP

▶ "Keep the ball as close to your body as you can when dribbling so that you always have it under control and can change direction at any time."

▶ "Always keep an eye on the position of the other players, even when dribbling. Look up, away from the ball."

▶ "Always use your body to shield the ball from a challenge by a player on the opposing team. In other words, block them out. This will make it easier to retain possession of the ball."

▶ "When dribbling with the intention of making a break or pass, keep the ball under control and keep moving at moderate speed. Dribbling too fast will make it harder to follow play."

▶ "Feigning an attack or changing speed or direction is a good way of dribbling through a defence and scoring a goal."

ORGANIZATIONAL TIPS

■ When the ball goes into touch, instead of a throw-in the ball is dribbled or passed onto the pitch from where it went into touch.

■ Where four or, with large training groups, six teams of four players can be formed, all the 4-man teams should play each other simultaneously on parallel pitches (in the form of a tournament).

■ Players belonging to any teams not currently involved in the tournament should be given simple, but interesting exercises focusing on the central aspect of the training session (e.g. slalom course, ball-skill exercises). After the next change-over, another 4-man team takes over.

INCREASE/DECREASE THE DIFFICULTY

■ **Easier/harder:**
The size of the pitch and goals should be adapted to the ability of the players. The larger the pitch, the easier it is to dribble, retain possession of the ball and play as a team.

■ **Harder:**
When a pass is received, the ball must first be brought under control and dribbled before being passed to a team-mate, otherwise the opposing team is awarded possession.

■ **Harder:**
After a goal, the scorer may only dribble the ball onto the pitch or pass to a team-mate from the goal line. In addition, the ball must cross the half-way line at least once before a goal can be scored between the markers on that same goal line.

■ **Harder:**
Individual (outstanding) players are not allowed to score themselves, but can only set up scoring opportunities for their team-mates as playmakers.

Variant 4:
End-to-end 4-a-side. Each team defends the two goals on its own goal line. When a goal has been scored, the opposing team is awarded possession of the ball.

Variant 5:
An extra goal – either marked out or a portable 5-metre goal – defended by a goalkeeper, is placed approximately 15 metres behind each goal line.
After dribbling through one of the small goals, the same player tries to score a second time by shooting at the extra goal.

After a goal has been scored, the goalkeeper gives the ball to a player on the opposing team. This player then dribbles the ball onto the pitch at any point and the 4-a-side game continues.

DRIBBLING

Soccer technique is never just an end in itself. Being able to dribble well is also an important prerequisite for solving problems that arise during play. For this reason, players should always be trained to dribble the ball in actual game situations.

HOW THE GAME WORKS

4-a-side with small goals in a grid

Three or four makeshift goals 2 metres wide (cones, poles, etc.) are set up at random on a pitch measuring about 25 x 25 metres. Two teams of four players each can score by dribbling the ball over one of the goal lines after a passing move.
The team scoring a goal remains in possession of the ball but must then attack a different goal.

Duration of the game:
2 to 4 minutes

Variant 1:
Other players (e.g. from one of the other 4-man teams) move down the touchlines ready to receive passes from the team in possession of the ball. It may make sense to limit the number of touches made by these additional players (e.g. one-touch play only).

Variant 2:
Where there are three 4-man teams, the players belonging to the team not involved in the game stand on the pitch with their legs wide apart to form four extra small goals. The two teams playing the game then aim to play the ball through their legs during the 4-a-side game.

Variant 3:
A ninth player participates in the team-play of the 4-man team currently on the attack.
Particularly where weaker teams are concerned, the coach, for example, can control the run of play by serving as the additional player ready to receive passes.

CORRECTIVE HELP

▶ "Use your body to shield the ball from your opponents when they try and dispossess you."
▶ "Feign a penetrating solo run on one side and then suddenly change both direction and speed and head for another goal."
▶ "To protect the ball, dribble into space away from players on the opposing team until a gap or passing opportunity is created."
▶ "Vary your dribbling by using both the inside and the outside of your feet. Change direction while dribbling to make your movements less predictable."
▶ "Dribble carefully, keeping the ball under control, but always keep an eye on what is going on around you. This will help you to recognize passing opportunities or gaps immediately."

ORGANIZATIONAL TIPS

■ When the ball goes into touch, a player from the opposing team has to dribble it back onto the pitch. This will make for a smoother run of play than restarting with a normal throw-in. It will also help to focus the players' attention on their dribbling technique.
■ Alternating between three teams of 4 players, with one team at a time performing special functions (e.g. receiving passes or acting as extra goals), is also a good way of spreading the workload evenly.
■ A few spare balls should be placed around the pitch to prevent long breaks in play from arising when balls are retrieved.
■ Where the game is played simultaneously on two or three pitches, the coach must be able to keep an eye on all the teams at the same time.

INCREASE/DECREASE THE DIFFICULTY

■ **Easier:**
If too few goals are scored through dribbling, the coach should widen the goals and/or set up additional small goals. The players must be guaranteed a sense of achievement.
■ **Easier:**
The attackers can dribble the ball off the pitch to protect against being dispossessed. They cannot be tackled when in touch.
■ **Easier:**
If there is too little dribbling and possession of the ball is constantly changing, make the pitch bigger. The more space individual players have to move around in, the easier ball control and accurate dribbling becomes.

Variant 4:
The players are divided into fixed pairs. The player in possession of the ball must then engage in a 1-on-1 situation with his partner before dribbling the ball through any goal markers. When choosing the pairs, make sure that the two players concerned are of roughly equal ability.

Variant 5:
Besides the small goals, a larger goal guarded by a goalkeeper is also set up on the pitch. Goals scored in this goal are counted the same as those scored by dribbling the ball through one of the small goals.

Variant 6:
Six makeshift goals (three marked by cones, three by poles) are set up at random on the pitch.
Team A has to score by dribbling the ball through a "pole goal", team B through a "cone goal."

DRIBBLING # 1

Variants:

■ Each player in a pair is allocated his own goal line. The player can score only in one of the three small goals along the other player's goal line.

■ Each pair plays 1-on-1 into two goals opposite each other, with the width of the goals increased to approximately 4 metres.

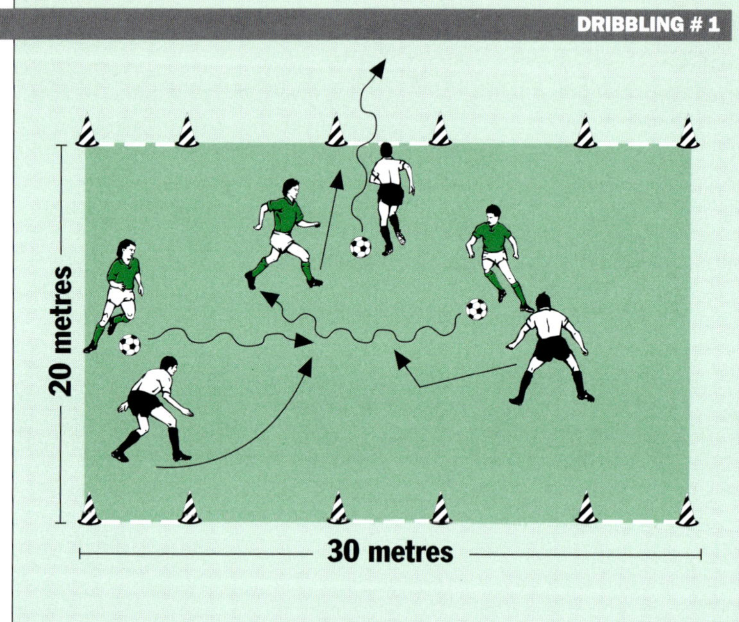

HOW THE TRAINING GAME WORKS

1-on-1 through different small goals

Three pairs play 1-on-1 on a pitch measuring 30 x 20 metres with three goals (3 metres wide) set up along each of the longer sides. The players score by dribbling the ball through any one of the six goals. The goalscorer remains in possession of the ball and cannot be tackled by players on the opposing team until he is back on the actual pitch. The next goal has to be scored through a different goal.

Duration of the game:
1 minute at the most

DRIBBLING # 2

Variants:

■ Which of the two players is the first to manage three successful return passes with the off-field players?

■ The attackers can only play return passes with the two passers from their own team.

■ After executing a return pass with one of the passers from his own team, the player on the pitch immediately trades places with the passer.

■ The passers are allowed no more than two touches of the ball.

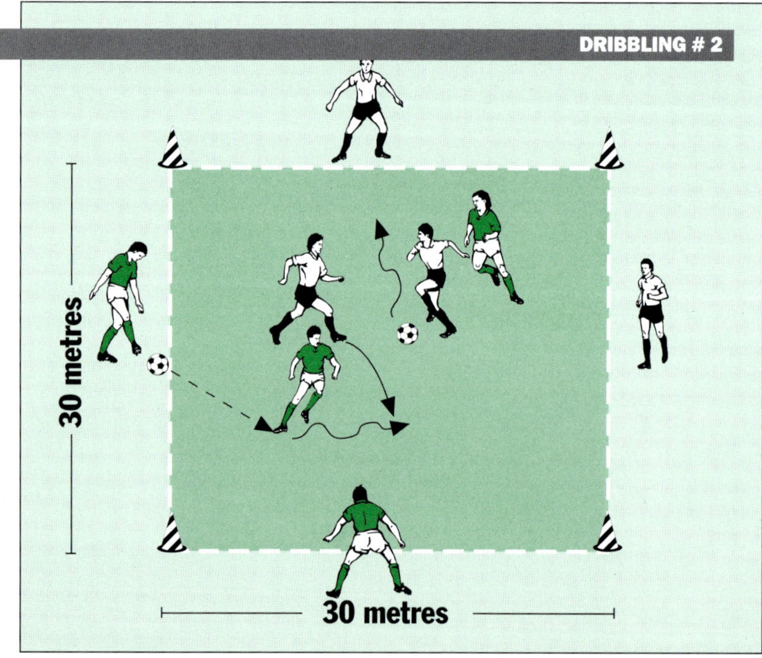

HOW THE TRAINING GAME WORKS

1-on-1: Staying in possession with the help of "passers"

On a pitch measuring 30 x 30 metres, two 4-man teams play 1-on-1 as follows:
Each player in team A is assigned a partner from team B. There are always two pairs of players on the pitch. The other four players make themselves available on the touchlines as passers of the ball.
Which player can remain in possession for longest by playing return passes with all four passers?

Duration of the game:
30 seconds to 1 minute

HOW THE TRAINING GAME WORKS

3 x 1-on-1 into goals

Two small goals 6 to 8 metres apart are set up on each of the goal lines of a pitch measuring approximately 20 x 25 metres. The trainer divides the group into two teams of equal size.
Three pairs (three players from each team) play 1-on-1, with the player in possession allowed to score in either of his opponent's goals.
The other players stand behind their own two goals and stop the balls. After 30 seconds, they trade with the players on the pitch, and so on.

DRIBBLING # 3

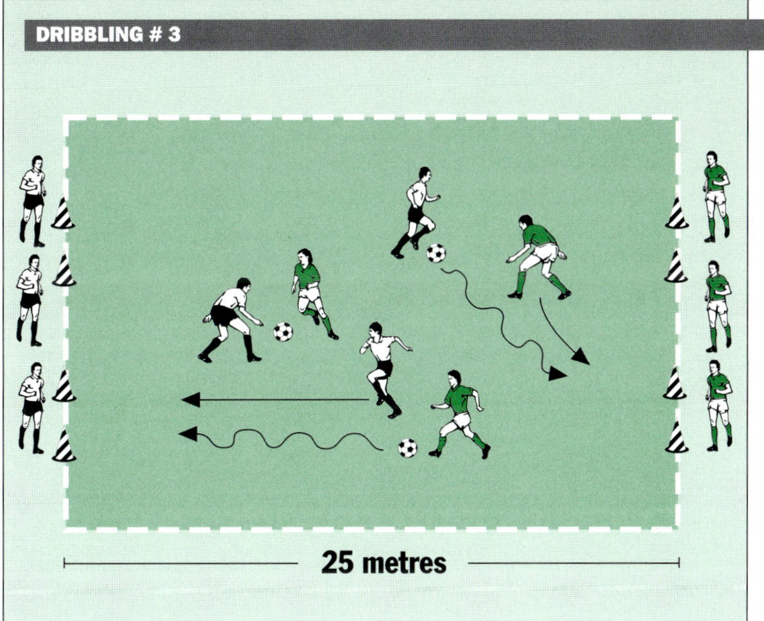

Variants:

- Same game, but played into goals 5 metres wide, guarded by goalkeepers. The players not currently involved in the 1-on-1 game take over as goalkeepers.
- With the teams awarded points: Any goals scored count for the team as a whole. The winning team is the one which has scored the most goals after a set time – or alternately the first team to score 20 goals.

HOW THE TRAINING GAME WORKS

3 x alternate 1-on-1 over target lines

Two groups of three players split up into three pairs to play 1-on-1 between two designated target lines. One pair then plays 1-on-1, with the attacker trying to dribble the ball across his opponent's target line. The other two pairs stand behind the target lines.
After dribbling the ball across the target line, the attacker passes it to his team-mate who sets off to play 1-on-1 against his opponent and tries to cross the line at the other end. The defending players are only allowed to tackle between the target lines.

DRIBBLING # 4

Variants:

- With points, a competition to see which group can cross the opponent's target line the most times in five minutes.
- The length of the target lines should be altered to match the players' ability.

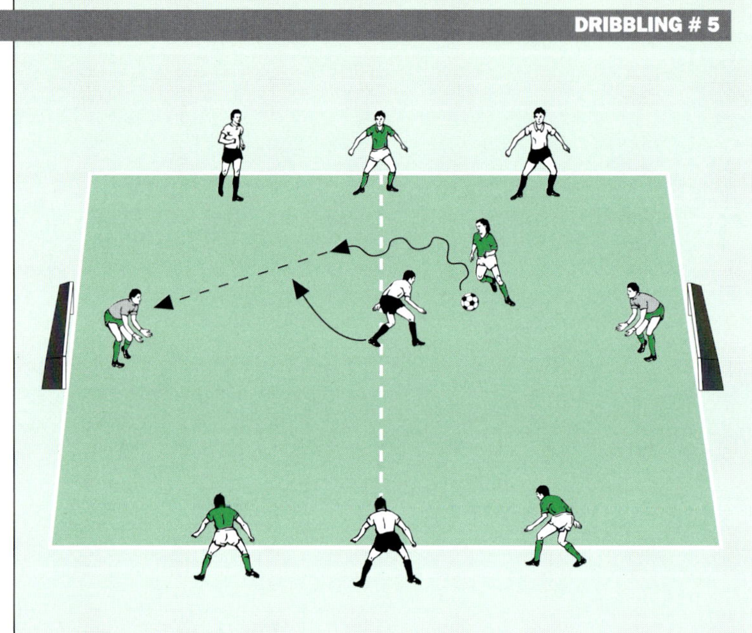

Variants:

- The passers are not allowed more than two touches of the ball.
- Players in possession of the ball can only combine with their three team-mates who are acting as passers on the touchlines.

HOW THE TRAINING GAME WORKS

1-on-1 into goals with "passers"

Two groups of four players are split into four pairs. On a pitch measuring about 20 x 25 metres, one of these pairs plays 1-on-1 into two goals guarded by goal-keepers. The players not involved spread out around the pitch and act as passers helping the attacker (even if he belongs to the other team).
After one minute, the next pair takes over.
The winners are the team which has scored the most goals after five individual pairings.

Variants:

- The attacker also has to dribble round the goal-keeper.
- The trainer stands behind the pitches with a number of balls and initiates each move by passing to the respective attacker.
- After each run-through (or after four to six moves), the attacking and defending players trade places.

HOW THE TRAINING GAME WORKS

1-on-1 in front of the penalty area

Three pitches each measuring about 10 x 12 metres are marked out directly in front of the penalty area with two players and one ball in each zone.
The following move then takes place in each pitch in succession: The attacker attempts, in a 1-on-1 situation, to get past the defending player and dribble the ball through the marked zone into the penalty area. Once he has done this, he can take a free shot at goal.

HOW THE TRAINING GAME WORKS

3-a-side in front of the penalty area

Two groups play 3-a-side on a pitch measuring approximately 40 x 30 metres and bordering directly on the penalty area.
The attackers have to combine to dribble the ball across line A into the penalty area. The player managing this is then allowed to take a free shot at goal.
On winning possession of the ball, the defending team must dribble the ball across line B. The two teams then switch positions.

DRIBBLING # 7

Variants:

- After scoring a goal, the same team starts a new attacking move from behind line B.
- The attacking team is strengthened by adding a neutral player.
- On winning possession of the ball, the defending players must counter by dribbling it through one of two small makeshift goals (cones) on line B.

HOW THE TRAINING GAME WORKS

1-on-1 from different positions

The players split up into attackers and defenders approximately 25 metres in front of a goal defended by a goalkeeper.
The idea is for the striker to dribble the ball round his opponent in a 1-on-1 situation and then shoot at goal. The pairs trade places every five to seven run-throughs.
The various attacks are launched from different directions towards the goal:

- 25 metres directly in front of the goal,
- from the left/right wing.

DRIBBLING # 8

Variants:

- After winning possession of the ball, the defending player has a chance to counter by playing the ball into one of two small "counter goals".
- The attackers and defenders stand next to each other on the goal line to one side of the goal. The attacker dribbles the ball into the penalty area and, with his opponent initially behind him, tries to score a goal.

PASSING – SUPPORT AND RUNNING INTO SPACE

Accurate passing constitutes the technical basis of all team-play. When teaching passing techniques in games and exercises, it is also important at the same time to work on tactical aspects, such as running into and using space.

BASIC GAME # 1

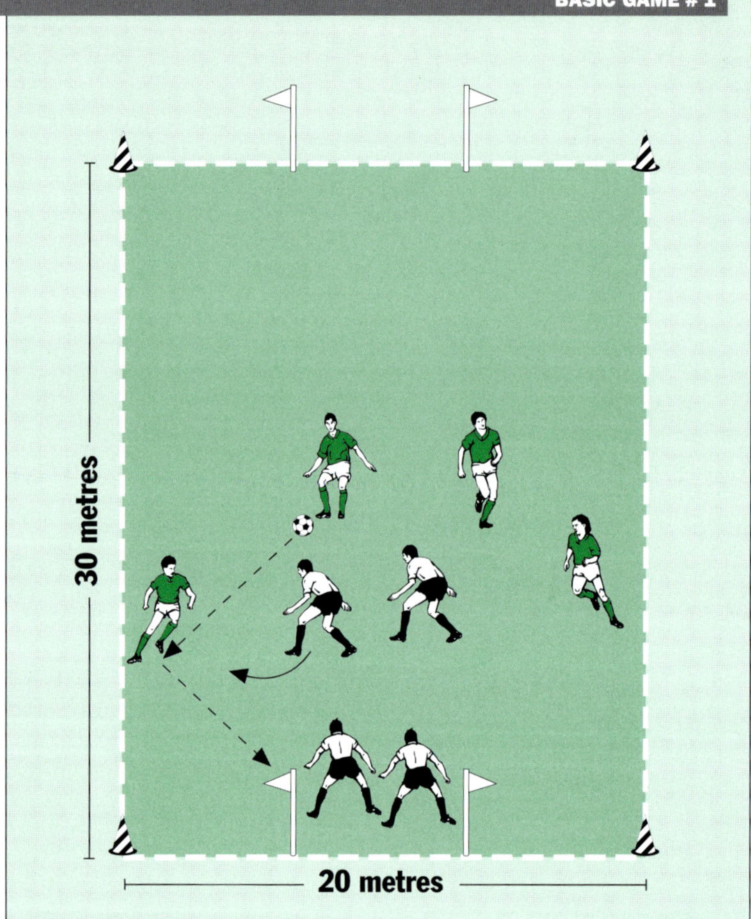

HOW THE GAME WORKS

4 against 2 + 2 goal-keepers into 2 goals

Two teams play 4-a-side into makeshift goals (poles) about 5 metres wide on a pitch measuring approximately 20 x 30 metres. Two players from the respective defending team take over as goal-keepers in their own goal, thereby creating a 4-against-2 attacking situation. After a shot at goal (whether successful or not) or when the ball has been won by the defending team the roles are reversed, with the previously defending team going on the attack, again in a 4-against-2 + 2 formation. The team now on the defensive may only try and regain possession of the ball when two of its players have taken up their positions as goalkeepers, otherwise the opposition is awarded a penalty.

Duration of the game: 5 minutes

Variant 1:
4 against 2 + 2 from goal line to goal line instead of into goals. To score, each team must combine to dribble the ball across the opposition's goal line. Two players on the defending team must wait behind their own goal line and may not interfere in the game. As soon as the defending team wins the ball, the two teams trade roles. However, the team now attacking must first pass the ball back to one of its two players standing behind the goal line.
At the same time, two players from the other team must retreat to behind their goal line.

Variant 2:
The teams do not switch roles after a goal has been scored. Instead, the next attack is launched by having one of the goalkeepers throw a ball to the player on the attacking team who is furthest away from him.

CORRECTIVE HELP

▶ "The safest, most accurate way of passing the ball is with the inside of the foot, because the instep offers the widest area of contact."

■ "On the other hand, a pass with the outside of the foot can be played extremely quickly."

■ "This form of 'concealed pass' is ideal, in particular, for quick surprise moves in tight spaces."

■ "When passing the ball using the inside of the foot, the ankle of the foot playing the ball is kept rigid with the tip of the boot pointing outwards and upwards. When playing the ball with the inside of the foot, the leg playing the ball swings back to gain momentum and then follows the ball through."

ORGANIZATIONAL TIPS

■ Sufficient spare balls should be kept ready at all the goals to avoid interrupting the game.

■ If there are no spare balls, one player from the defending team stands on the goal line as goalkeeper and another a few metres behind the goal to stop the ball.

■ Makeshift goals should be positioned in such a way that obstacles behind the goals can stop the balls (wire-mesh fence, pitch barriers, etc.).

■ Goals formed using poles are always better for shooting games than cones, because they give an indication of the agreed height of the goal.

INCREASE/DECREASE THE DIFFICULTY

■ **Easier/harder:**
The size of the pitch and goals should be adapted to the players' ability.

■ **Easier/harder:**
Where there are excessive differences in ability level within the training group, 4-man teams comprising players of more or less equal ability should be formed for the pairings, each of which can then play under easier or harder conditions (different pitch and goal sizes, different rules, etc.).

■ **Harder:**
Differences in teams' strength can also be ironed out by making life harder for the stronger team, e.g. making it continue to play with two goalkeepers while stipulating that the weaker team only has to have one.

Variant 3:
Two 5-metre wide goals comprising poles are set up next to each other about 10 metres apart on each goal line of a slightly widened pitch.
Each of these goals is guarded by a player belonging to the defending team. The attacking team can score in any goal in the 4-against-2 situation.

Variant 4:
Same as Variant 3 except that the width of the goals is increased to 8 metres. The attackers now have to dribble the ball through the goals. The two "goalkeepers" may not leave their goal when trying either to prevent players from scoring or attempting to gain possession of the ball.

PASSING – SUPPORT AND RUNNING INTO SPACE

The main priority is for players to learn to identify exactly when passes should be played and always to pass the ball accurately. This is essential for safe team-play.

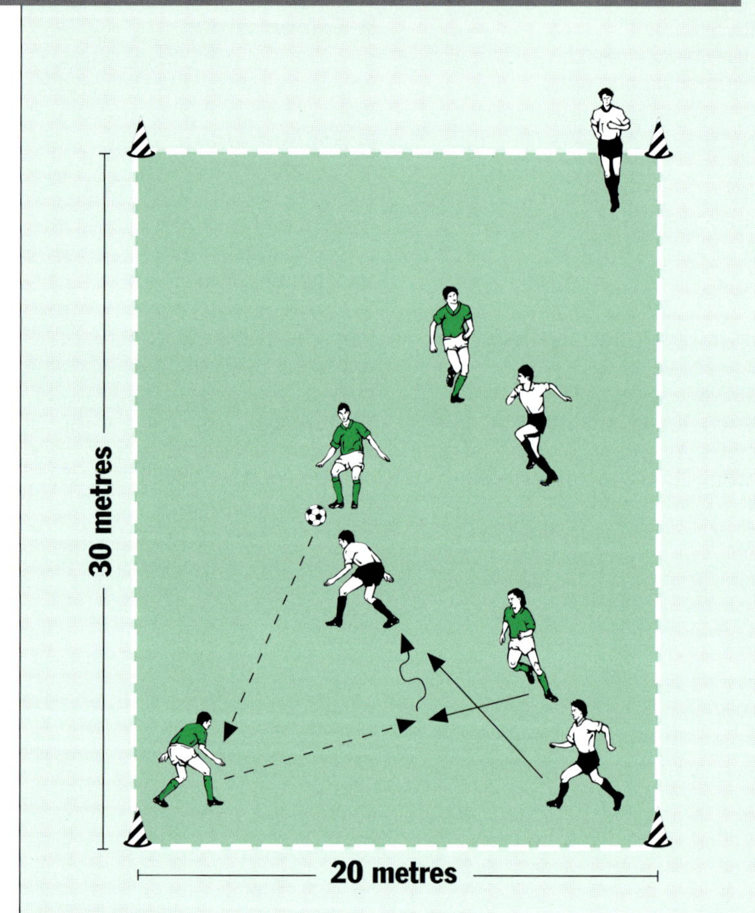

HOW THE GAME WORKS

4-a-side with 3-against-3 and each side having one substitute on the pitch

Two teams play 4-a-side on a pitch measuring about 20 x 30 metres. The aim of the game is to keep possession of the ball. One player on each team is confined to a corner of the pitch as a passer. The team with the ball must now stay in possession as long as possible in a 3-against-3 situation, passing the ball about between themselves and their own side's passer.
The passers may not be tackled directly.
From time to time, the game is interrupted to allow a different player to take over the role of passer.

Duration of the game: approximately 5 minutes

Variant 1:
The player passing to the passer has to trade places with him immediately.

Variant 2:
In addition, "points" are now awarded as follows:
One point is awarded for five consecutive passes within a team. The passer should be involved in these sequences as often as possible. The winner is the team with the most points at the end of the game.

Variant 3:
One point is awarded for each pass to a team's own passer followed by the two players concerned trading positions. The successful team keeps possession of the ball but at least two more passes must be made between its three more mobile players before another point can be scored.

CORRECTIVE HELP

▶ "Pass the ball to your team-mate's feet whenever possible. This will help him bring the ball under control more quickly."
▶ "Wherever possible, pass safely and accurately to the passer. This avoids risky 1-on-1 situations."
▶ "When running into space, remain in visual contact with your team-mate on the ball. Shake off any opposing defenders so that he can pass to you safely."
▶ "Playing safe passes at an easy pace makes it easier to follow play."
▶ "Use the entire pitch, making it more difficult for the opposition to gain possession of the ball."

ORGANIZATIONAL TIPS

■ Games for improving passing are particularly suitable for indoor training as even floors make for precise passes.
■ On uneven floors, the degree of difficulty of the exercise should be reduced if longer passing combinations prove impossible.
■ Where two or three pitches are occupied at the same time, they should be positioned in such a way that the coach can keep his eye on as many of the players as possible.
■ Sufficient spare balls must be kept ready at the corners of the pitch to avoid long breaks in play.

INCREASE/DECREASE THE DIFFICULTY

■ **Easier:**
The two passers are allowed to move around across the entire width of the base line. The idea is for them to run into space to make a safe target for passes.
■ **Easier:**
The coach can strengthen the team in possession by acting as an additional player.
■ **Harder:**
Players are allowed to tackle the passers.
■ **Harder:**
The number of touches allowed for the passers can be limited, where necessary to one touch, according to the players' ability.

Variant 4:
The same as Variant 3 except that the pitch is now divided by a half-way line marked with cones.
Passes from the far half of the pitch to a team's own passer, followed by successfully trading positions, score double points.

Variant 5:
Passes between the more mobile players may not exceed hip height, otherwise the opposing team is given possession of the ball.

Variant 6:
3-a-side plus two passers:
The team in possession of the ball can now play using both passers. After passing to his own team's passer, the player who made the pass trades positions with him. If he passes to his "partner" from the opposing team he stays where he is, in the "outfield."

PASSING – SUPPORT AND RUNNING INTO SPACE

Passes played with the inside or outside of the foot are used particularly in tight spaces. The safest, most accurate way of passing is using the inside of the foot.

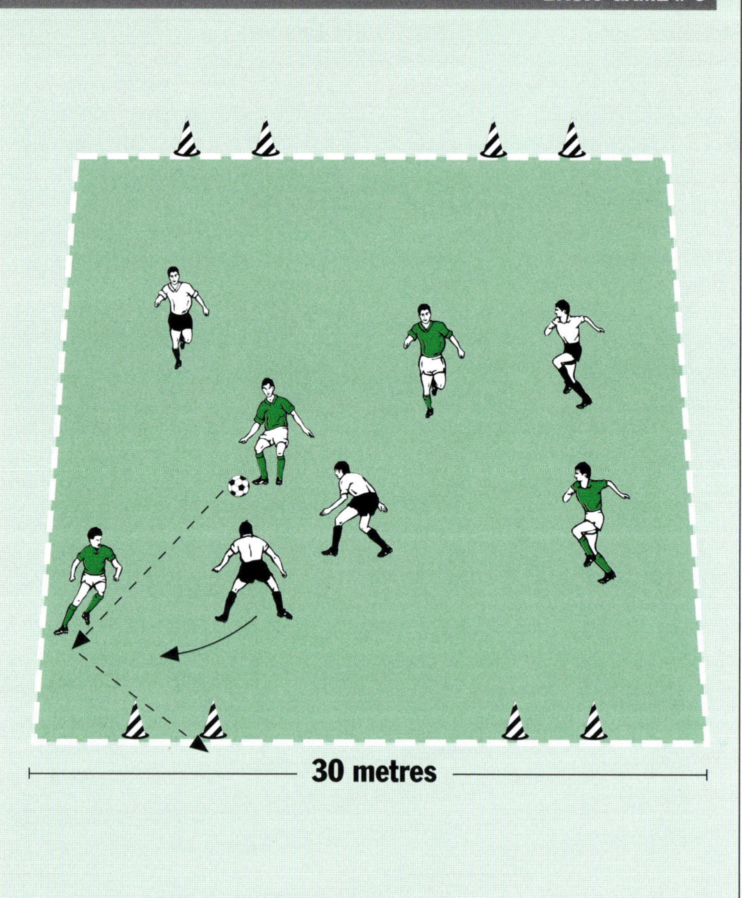

HOW THE GAME WORKS

4-a-side into four small goals

Two makeshift goals (poles, cones) are set up on each goal line of a pitch measuring about 30 x 20 metres.
To score, the players have to make a precise pass through one of the four goals while playing 4-a-side.
Any team scoring a goal retains possession of the ball. To continue the game, the goalscorer can dribble the ball back onto the pitch or pass to a team-mate from any point off the pitch.
The next goal has to be scored in one of the other three goals.
The defending players can only gain possession of the ball on the pitch.

Duration of the game: 5 minutes

Variant 1:
Any team scoring a goal must subsequently attack one of the goals on the other goal line to score again.

Variant 2:
Each 4-man team is assigned two goals diagonally opposite each other to defend.
This makes suddenly shifting play even more important when trying to score.

Variant 3:
As in Variant 2 except that the game is played around the two opposing goals. Goals can be scored from either side.
Since this variant makes the players do a great deal of running, the duration of the game should be reduced to about three minutes.

CORRECTIVE HELP

➤ "Play fast but safe passing combinations. This is the only way to outwit players on the other team."
➤ "Unexpected shifts in play can create goal-scoring opportunities in front of another goal, so practise suddenly changing the direction of your run or play."
➤ "Make yourselves available on the far side of the ball at the right time so that play can be shifted after just a few passes."
➤ "After successfully switching play, go for goal single-mindedly. Don't give the opposition's defence time to re-group."
➤ "Make yourself available for passes at the back so that the direction of play can be changed safely."

ORGANIZATIONAL TIPS

■ To avoid long interruptions, as many spare balls as possible should be kept ready near all the goals before the start of the game.
■ In addition, the pitches should be set out in such a way that obstacles behind the small goals (e.g. pitch barriers, fencing, etc.) stop the balls from rolling away.
■ In some cases, the coach might find it convenient to stand behind the goal to observe the game and stop the balls himself.
■ Competitions between the two teams in shooting accuracy are a very good way of actively using the breaks between individual run-throughs of the game.

INCREASE/DECREASE THE DIFFICULTY

■ **Easier:**
The coach (or an extra player) acts as a "neutral" player, helping out the team in possession of the ball in attack (5-against-4 situation).
■ **Easier:**
Making the pitch bigger gives individual players more room to move around in and eases the opposition's pressure on the player in possession of the ball, increasing the time available to start off a new move. A larger pitch thus facilitates controlled, safe team-play.
■ **Easier:**
Widening the goals is another way of giving weaker players a taste of success.
■ **Harder:**
Each pass must be brought under control and moved along before it can be passed to another player. Only shots at goal can be taken first-time.
■ **Harder:**
In game variants with two goals a side, goals may only be scored by players in the opposing team's half.

Variant 4:
As in Variant 1 except that the two teams are given different instructions. Team A has to pass the ball through one of the opposition's goals while team B has to dribble the ball through. After the end of the first game and a break, the teams then trade around.

Variant 5:
Team A plays into two larger opposing goals defended by goalkeepers set up on the same goal line, while team B plays into two small goals formed using cones. After the first game and an active break, the teams switch round. The winner is the team with the most goals at the end of the game.

Variant 6:
Each 4-man team defends one large goal guarded by a goalkeeper and one small goal on the same goal line. During attacking moves by the opposing team, one player has to go into the large goal as goalkeeper (a 4-against-3 attacking situation).

Variants:

- The number of touches of the ball allowed is adapted to match the players' ability.
- 5-against-2 game.
- Which team can manage 10 consecutive passes?
- After 10 consecutive passes by the attackers, the "infield players" are made to stay in the middle for an "additional round."

HOW THE TRAINING GAME WORKS

4 against 2

On a pitch measuring about 10 x 15 metres, four attackers play as "outfield players" (around the edges of the pitch) against two "infield" defenders.
The idea is for the attackers to keep possession of the ball with no player allowed more than three touches of the ball before passing - as safely and accurately as possible. When a defending player gains possession of the ball, the "infield player" who has been in the middle of the pitch for longest moves to the periphery. The attacker who caused possession of the ball to be lost then becomes a defender.

PASSING – SUPPORT AND RUNNING INTO SPACE # 2

Variants:

- The number of touches of the ball allowed before the next pass can be limited for the attacking team where the level of ability is appropriate.
- Playing with dedicated goalkeepers:
2 players from the defending team are goalkeepers, thus resulting once again in a 4-against-2 attacking situation.

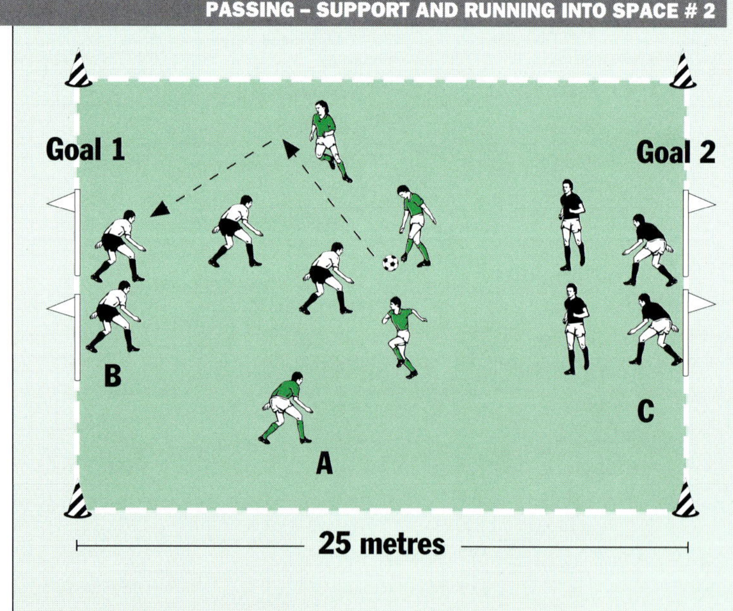

HOW THE TRAINING GAME WORKS

4-against-2 + 2 goalkeepers with three teams

Two goals (5 metres wide) marked using poles are set up on the goal lines of a pitch measuring around 20 x 25 metres. Two out of three 4-man teams play against each other between these goals, alternating as follows:
Team A attacks team B by attacking goal number 1. Two players from team B go into goal, thus resulting in a 4-against-2 attacking situation. Team C waits by goal number 2 with two goalkeepers and two defenders. After winning possession of the ball in front of goal number 1, team B then goes on the attack against team C by attacking goal number 2.

PASSING – SUPPORT AND RUNNING INTO SPACE # 3

HOW THE TRAINING GAME WORKS

4-a-side with two "passers" on the sidelines, attacking two goals guarded by goalkeepers

Two goals guarded by goalkeepers are set up on the goal lines of a pitch measuring about 40 x 30 metres. The trainer forms two 6-man teams. Four players from each team play 4-a-side, attacking the two goals. The two remaining players of each team move up and down the sidelines of the opposing team's half, acting as additional passers and cannot be tackled. The players trade places within the team after a set time.

30 metres

Variants:

- The passers are restricted to two touches or even instructed to play the ball first-time.
- All four passers along the sidelines belong to the team in possession of the ball.

PASSING – SUPPORT AND RUNNING INTO SPACE # 4

HOW THE TRAINING GAME WORKS

3-against-3 + 1 between 2 "passers"

Three 3-man teams practice together on a pitch measuring 20 x 30 metres. Teams A and B play 3-a-side within the confines of the pitch while two players from group C stand behind the base lines as passers. During the 3-a-side game, the 3-man team in possession of the ball must combine as often as possible with the passers on the base lines, helped by the third player from group C who acts as an on-field passer.

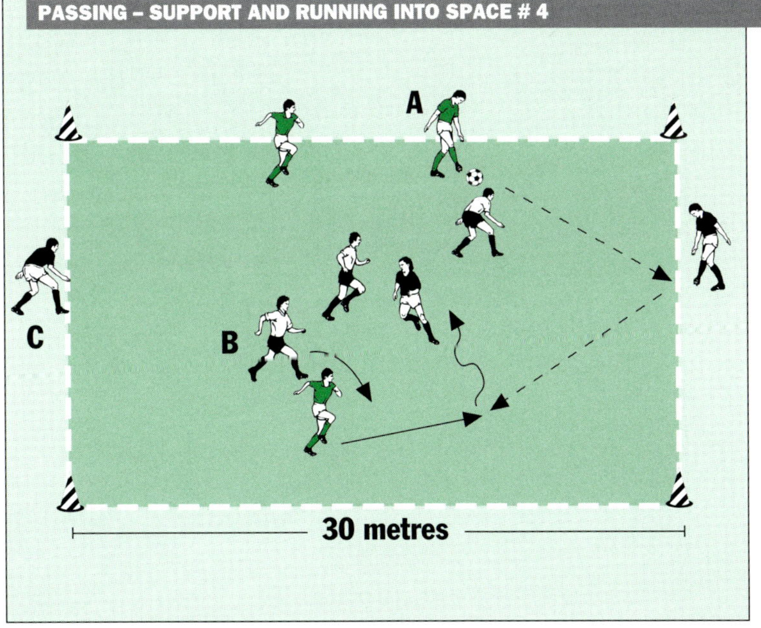

Variants:

- Points are awarded as follows:
  1 point to the team in possession of the ball for each passing combination between passers.
- The passers are restricted to a certain number of touches of the ball.

BALL CONTROL

Players need to learn how to bring the ball under control when they receive a low, slightly lofted or high pass, even when they are under pressure. They must then play the ball with purpose and determination.

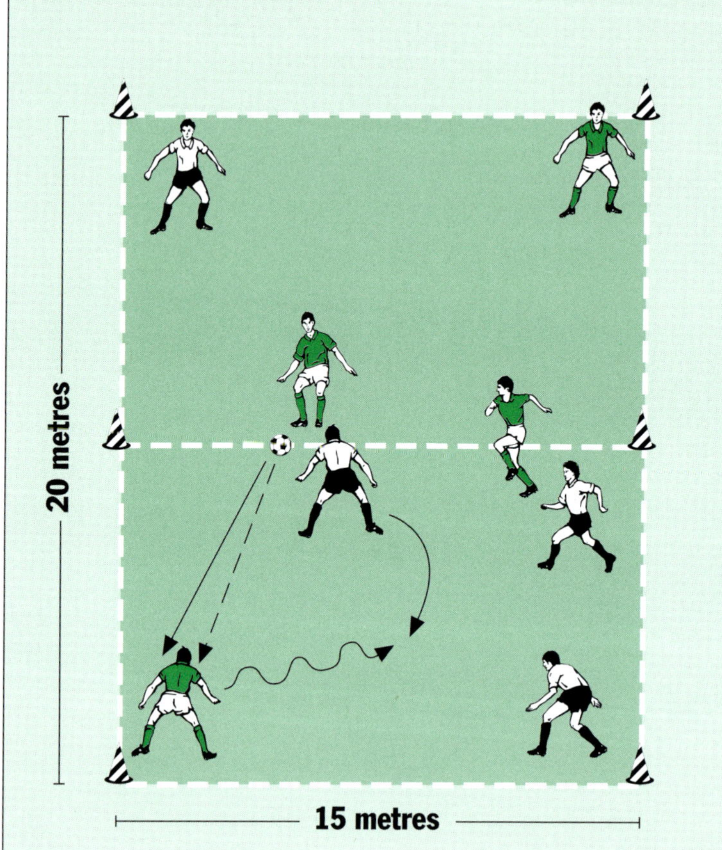

HOW THE GAME WORKS

2-against-2 + 2 substitutes each

The pitch, measuring about 15 x 20 metres, is divided in two by a half-way line. From two 4-man teams, two players each play 2-against-2 while the other two players on each team initially wait in the corners of the pitch as substitutes – with the two substitutes who are team-mates standing diagonally opposite each other.
The idea in the 2-against-2 game is to keep possession of the ball for as long as possible. A player who has passed to one of his team's two substitutes immediately trades places with him.
1 point is awarded for five successive passes played by the 4-man team.

Duration of the game: max. 4 minutes

Variant 1:
Each pass must first be controlled and the ball moved along before the player can lay off the ball again.
If a player plays the ball first-time, the opposition is awarded possession of the ball.

Variant 2:
To score a point by making five successive passes, at least one substitute player has to be involved.
However, the substitutes may now move freely all the way around the touchline.

Variant 3:
The two passers on each 4-man team stand in the corners of the opponents' half.
The teams can now only score points by passing to one of their own team's passers from their own half of the pitch.

CORRECTIVE HELP

▶ "On making contact with the ball, take the 'sting' out of the pass using your foot."
▶ "Raise your foot slightly to prevent the from ball rolling over it or bouncing away."
▶ "Take the ball on the move and play it into space. This will make keeping possession easier."
▶ "Whenever you can, combine ball control with a body feint. That way, you can shake off your marker and avoid tackles."
▶ "Involve the passers in the game continually. This will make keeping possession easier."
▶ "Spread out and make yourselves available over the entire pitch. That way you will create more space for yourselves and make it easier to keep the ball under control."

ORGANIZATIONAL TIPS

■ As this game makes substantial technical and tactical demands on young players, the ground must not be too uneven. If the ball keeps bouncing awkwardly, reduce the level of difficulty accordingly.
The players will only taste success and feel they have learnt something when a team can retain possession of the ball for a number of passes.
■ If the game is played on several pitches simultaneously, they should be set out in such a way that the coach can keep his eye on all the players.
In this way, he can recognize any problems that need ironing out and offer some assistance straight away.

INCREASE/DECREASE THE DIFFICULTY

■ **Easier:**
The bigger the pitch, the easier ball control and team-play become.
■ **Easier:**
Allowing the substitutes more room to move around in (e.g. up and down the full length of the touchline) gives the player on the ball better passing possibilities, thus making it easier for the team to retain possession.
■ **Easier/harder:**
The number of touches of the ball in succession required to score a point can be adapted to match the teams' ability with a view to guaranteeing the required sense of achievement (i.e. scoring points).

Variant 4:
All variants can also be played in the form of a 3-a-side game with only one passer in a corner of the pitch (or on the touchline). If so, the pitch should be made bigger.

Variant 5:
For weaker teams, the coach (or one of the stronger players) can help the two players of the team in possession of the ball, acting as an additional team-mate.

Variant 6:
Only low passes (no more than hip height) are allowed, otherwise the opposing team is awarded possession of the ball. This additional rule underscores the key point about "safe team-play."

BALL CONTROL

Particularly in attacking situations, players must combine ball control with a body feint to shake off their markers and break through to take a shot at goal. Furthermore, upon receiving a pass, players must immediately bring the ball under control and then play it into space away from their marker.

HOW THE GAME WORKS

Shooting at goal after a safe build-up of play

The game is played over the entire width of one half of a standard pitch. In the middle between the goals (with goalkeepers), a 20 metre zone is marked out in which two groups play 4-a-side.
The idea is for the team in possession of the ball to shoot at goal after building up a good, safe move. To do this, it must first string together five consecutive passes and then have one player dribble the ball across one of the lines at the far end of the demarcated centre zone. Having done this, the player may take a free shot at goal. He must then immediately run back into the centre zone where his team has already started building up the next move with a second ball.

Duration of the game: 5 minutes

Variant 1:
After dribbling across the line at the edge of the centre zone, the attacker must beat the goalkeeper by himself in order to score.
He then immediately runs back to the centre zone.

Variant 2:
The coach positions himself in front of one of the goals to play wall passes. The attacker must now first play a one-two with the trainer before shooting at goal. The other goal continues to be attacked in the normal manner.

Variant 3:
Two goals approximately 5 metres wide are set up on each of the lines at the ends of the demarcated centre zone. Once a move has successfully been built up, an attacker has to dribble the ball through one of these "off-centre" goals before laying the ball back in front of the goal for a team-mate to take a free shot.

CORRECTIVE HELP

▶ "When you receive a pass, immediately bring the ball under control and then play it into space away from your marker. This way, you will avoid a risky 1-on-1 situation from the outset."
▶ "Run towards the ball to prevent your marker from reaching it before you do."
▶ "When receiving a pass, keep the ball under control and close to your body by using your foot to take the 'sting' out of it. That way, you will prevent the ball from spinning off your foot."
▶ "When controlling the ball, point the tip of your boot upwards slightly. This will stop the ball rolling over your foot or jumping up."
▶ "When receiving a pass, make a feint with your body in an effort to shake off your marker. This will give you more space to play a safe pass yourself."

ORGANIZATIONAL TIPS

■ Sufficient spare balls should be kept close to the centre zone to avoid any long interruptions of the game which will substantially reduce the effectiveness of the exercise and dampen the players' motivation.
■ If there are not enough goalkeepers, shooting at goal can be replaced by, say, target-shooting at a smaller goal.
■ This game requires a relatively large amount of space. If the other players have to be kept occupied at the same time, the coach will need an entire sports field.

INCREASE/DECREASE THE DIFFICULTY

■ **Easier:**
Enlarging the centre zone will make ball control and safe teamplay easier.
■ **Easier:**
Where weaker groups are concerned, the coach can also play in the centre zone, acting as an additional "neutral" player to help the team in possession of the ball build up a safe move.
■ **Easier:**
During the build-up of play, one player from each 4-man team is only allowed to move up and down the touchline of the centre zone and may not be tackled directly by the opposing team. His teammates can retain possession of the ball easier by passing to this "winger" when under pressure.
■ **Harder:**
Where stronger teams are concerned, the number of uninterrupted consecutive passes can be increased from five to seven (or 10) before a player can attack the goal.

Variant 4:
Goals are again set up on the long lines demarcating the centre zone. This time, an attacker must break through one of these goals and then pull the ball back, crossing it into the main goal area to a team-mate following him up. This team-mate may then score with a header or a volley.

Variant 5:
Points can also be awarded for all the game variants as follows: 1 point for each successful build-up (five consecutive touches of the ball), 1 additional point for a subsequent goal.

Variant 6:
After a successful build-up, the attackers may try to break through the "off-centre" goals or through the centre. A different shot at goal then has to be played, depending on the route taken. Goals scored after a breakthrough down the wing can also count double.

HOW THE TRAINING GAME WORKS

Passes from two "passers"

This game is played in groups of four, with two players moving around on a pitch measuring 10 x 10 metres. The other two players each have a ball and act as passers, each positioned about 5 metres behind a base line. The passers each play simultaneous low passes to their player moving on the pitch, who smartly brings the ball under control and moves it along before passing the ball on to the other passer.
The players trade places after every 10 run-throughs.

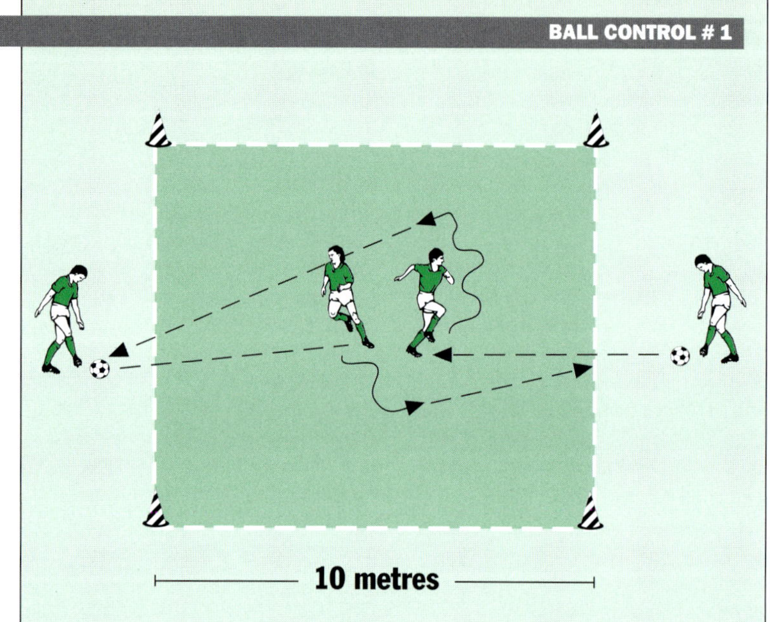

Variants:

- The players on the pitch receive virtually square passes and must then control the ball in a direction opposite to their run, moving towards the ball.
- The ball played in is slightly lofted (or thrown in).
- Each attempt to control the ball must be combined with a body feint.
- Only one ball is used. 1-on-1 on the pitch: the attacker has to run into space, control a pass and then feed it to the other passer.

HOW THE TRAINING GAME WORKS

2-against-2 in various directions of play

Two groups of four play on a pitch measuring 20 x 20 metres. Two players on each team are on the pitch itself, while the other two take up positions behind opposite base lines.
In a 2-against-2 situation on the pitch, the pair in possession of the ball tries to pass first to one of its passers and then to the other one; 1 point is awarded for each successful combination from 1 passer to another.

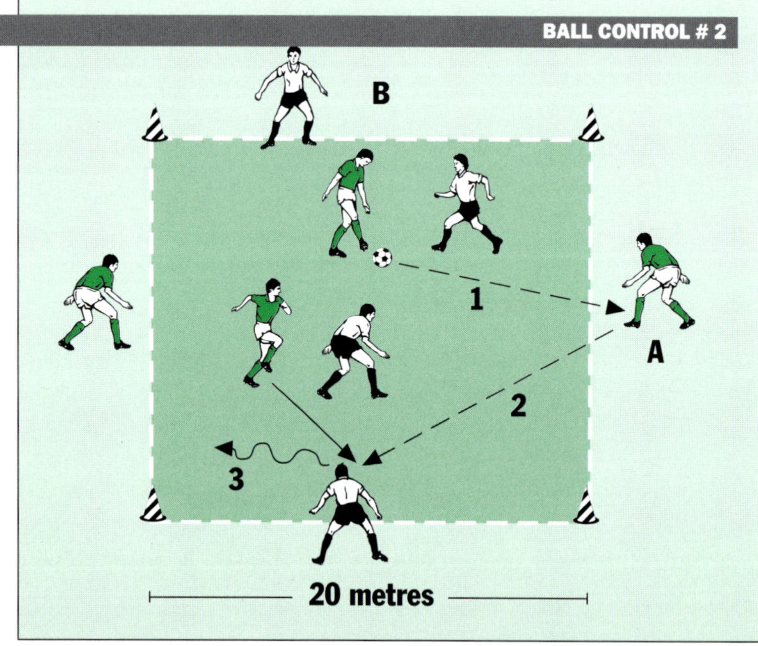

Variants:

- The team in possession of the ball is awarded one additional point for every five consecutive passes.
- The passers are only allowed to touch the ball a limited number of times.
- Places and tasks within the team are traded every two minutes. The winner is the team which has scored the most points after trading places three times.

HOW THE TRAINING GAME WORKS

3-a-side with three "throwers" into one goal guarded by a goalkeeper

Three groups of three play in front of a goal guarded by a goalkeeper. Groups A (attackers) and B (defenders) play 3-a-side inside the penalty area. The players in group C stand next to each other holding balls just outside the penalty area. The first "thrower" from group C throws a high ball to a player from group A who is making himself available and who then tries to go it alone and score a goal or score after combining with his team-mates. Once the attack has been completed, the second "thrower" starts off the next move.

BALL CONTROL # 3

Variants:

- When the defenders win the ball, they must pass it to the last "thrower." They are awarded 1 point for this.
The winner is the group with most points after 10 run-throughs.
- The attackers may play the ball back to the "thrower" if the attack breaks down. The same "thrower" then throws a high ball to one of the attackers again.
- After winning a ball and passing it to the "thrower" in question, the defenders trade places with the attackers.

HOW THE TRAINING GAME WORKS

Quick ball control, moving towards the goal

One player stands 5 metres outside the penalty area, acting as the first attacker. The others, each with a ball, stand behind each other about 35 metres away from the goal. The first player in the group plays a low pass to the attacker, who plays the ball a short distance towards the goal (with goalkeeper) and then shoots.
At the same time, the player passing the ball runs into the attacker's position ready to receive a pass from the next player, and so on.

BALL CONTROL # 4

Variants:

- The ball is controlled and pushed on using the inside of the foot.
- The ball is controlled and pushed on using the outside of the foot.
- The ball is controlled and pushed on while the player performs a simultaneous body feint.
- The player passing the ball follows it up and pressures the attacker by acting as a defender.
- The winner is the attacker who has scored the most goals by the end of the exercise.

SHOOTING AT GOAL

Naturally, shooting at goal is what every soccer player enjoys most. For this reason, particularly in the younger age groups, as many games and exercises as possible should include taking shots at goal. Nonetheless, from time to time the coach must also include special games designed to improve shooting technique.

BASIC GAME # 1

HOW THE GAME WORKS

4-a-side into one goal with a goalkeeper and a "counter-line"

A "counter-line" about 25 metres long is marked out roughly 25 metres away from a goal guarded by a goalkeeper.
Two groups play a game of 4-a-side between the goal and the "counter-line."
The idea is for team A to play a safe combination of passes leading up to a successful shot at goal. Team B disrupts the attacking move and, after winning the ball, launches a counter-attack, crossing the "counter-line."
As soon as a player from team B has dribbled the ball across the "counter-line", the teams trade places.
The winners are the team ending up with the most goals.

Duration of the game: 5 minutes

Variant 1:
After a goal or miss, the same team retains possession of the ball. It then launches a new attack, but from behind the "counter-line."
The defenders may only gain possession of the ball on the pitch itself.

Variant 2:
Here, the "counter-line" is replaced by two makeshift goals (cones or poles) about 3 metres wide. The players trade places when the defending team has dribbled or passed the ball through one of the two small goals in a counter-attack.

Variant 3:
If there is no goalkeeper available one player from the defending team acts as a goalkeeper, creating a situation in which there are four attackers playing against three defenders.
However, when the goalkeeper's team wins possession of the ball, he can take part in the counter-attack.

CORRECTIVE HELP

▶ "Take every opportunity to shoot."

▶ "Shoot from any promising situation. No shot – no goal."

▶ "Using the instep results in the most powerful shots. Position the pivot leg next to the ball, tensing the ankle of the kicking leg and keeping the tip of your boot pointing towards the ground."

▶ "Don't pass the ball again if you are in a promising shooting position. By doing so you would give the opposing team a chance to prevent the shot or even win back the ball."

▶ "Don't wait for the ball – always run towards a pass. That way, the players on the opposing team will have much less time to put you off or even block your shot."

ORGANIZATIONAL TIPS

■ Once again, as many spare balls as possible should be kept ready by the goal and behind the "counter-line" to avoid lengthy interruptions.

■ Alternatively, add a rule specifying that any balls missing the goal should be recovered by a player on the attacking team. While the ball is being recovered, the game continues with a second ball.

■ Again, makeshift goals (marked out by posts) should be set up in such a way that obstacles (advertising hoardings, nets) as close behind the goals as possible can stop the balls.

■ Where possible, additional pitches should be laid out parallel to each other so that balls from missed shots do not end up on another pitch.

INCREASE/DECREASE THE DIFFICULTY

■ **Easier:**
The coach (or another player) can join the attacking team as an additional passer at the back of the pitch. This will facilitate safe attacking build-up play and shooting opportunities.
The passer may not score goals himself.

■ **Easier:**
If there is no chance of a breakthrough and the attack breaks down, the ball may be played back behind the "counter-line" and a new attack built up from there. Attackers cannot be tackled behind the "counter-line."

■ **Harder:**
Make the pitch smaller, with the penalty area line becoming the "counter line." Reducing the space steps up the pressure on the attackers by making the offensive build-up and shooting more difficult.

Variant 4:
An additional semicircle with a radius of approximately 10 metres is marked out in front of the goal. Goals scored from outside this zone count double.

Variant 5:
No "counter-line": when the defending players gain possession of the ball, the teams immediately switch roles. However, the new attacking team cannot shoot until the ball has been passed at least once. This stops goals being picked up on the rebound.

Variant 6:
Goals resulting from first-time shots following sideways or pulled-back passes count double.
This provides the players with an incentive to stagger their attacks and intelligently lay the ball off to a team-mate after a breakthrough.

SHOOTING AT GOAL

If you don't shoot, you can't score. For this reason, the players must show courage and be prepared to take risks by resolutely snapping up any promising shooting opportunities. Coaches must constantly encourage their youngsters to do this during training and play.

BASIC GAME # 2

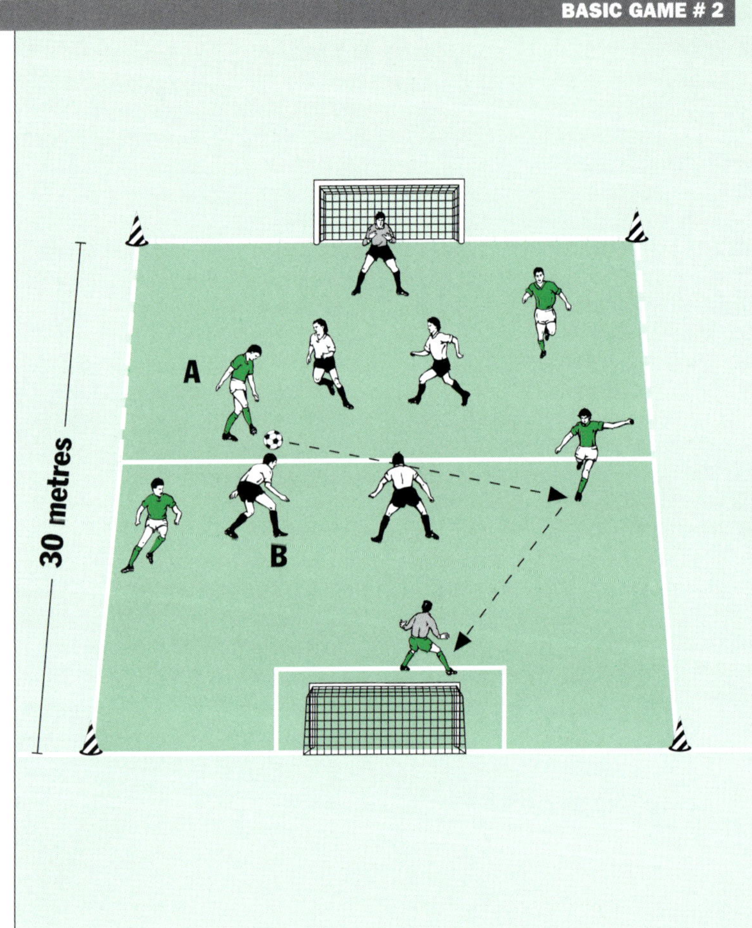

HOW THE GAME WORKS

4-a-side: shooting at goal versus retaining possession

Two goals, each guarded by a neutral goalkeeper, are positioned on the goal lines of a pitch measuring 40 x 30 metres, on which two teams play 4-a-side. The idea is for team A to score as many goals as possible in five minutes, attacking both goals. Team B tries to stop them by winning the ball and then retaining possession.

After a goal is scored, team A remains in possession. However, before it can launch another attack, it must play the ball across the half-way line at least once.

A break of roughly three minutes is taken after five minutes of play (and used to give the players tips or set them easy technical exercises).

The two teams then switch round. The winner is the team which has scored the most goals at the end of the game.

Variant 1:
After each shot at goal – whether successful or not – the attacking team retains possession of the ball. This encourages the players to be more adventurous and show greater determination in their shooting. However, before launching a fresh attack at goal, the ball must cross the half-way line at least once.

Variant 2:
The attackers may only attack the two goals alternately. The direction of the attack is changed after each shot, regardless of whether or not it was successful.

Variant 3:
Here, the defending team tries to retain possession of the ball and scores 1 point for every five consecutive passes.
The goals/points scored by the attackers and defenders are added together for each team.

CORRECTIVE HELP

▶ "Try to create shooting opportunities by passing the ball quickly and accurately."
▶ "A sudden, unexpected change in the direction of attack can set up a promising overlap situation in front of one of the goals."
▶ "Pass the ball to your team-mates so that they can run onto the pass and shoot first-time."
▶ "Move in such a way that the attack can be continued quickly and safely."
▶ "Deliberately dribble into space. Use body feints and changes of direction."
▶ "Run into space so that your team-mate can pass the ball either sideways or forwards."
▶ "Look for a shooting opportunity in any promising situation."

ORGANIZATIONAL TIPS

■ As before, keep spare balls ready near both goals.
■ The break between the two run-throughs must be long enough to allow the players to catch their breath so that the play and shooting action can be carried out at maximum speed and with full concentration. This is the only way to ensure that the young players will retain what they have learned in the long term.
■ Where there are three teams but no goalkeeper, the team taking a break provides the goalkeepers.
■ Where there are three teams but no goalkeeper, the team taking a break provides the goalkeepers.

INCREASE/DECREASE THE DIFFICULTY

■ Easier:
The two goalkeepers may not interfere with the passing moves strung together by the team with the ball.
■ Easier:
The coach serves as an additional passer for the team in possession of the ball (or only for the attacking team or the team trying to keep possession).
■ Easier:
Two players from the team attempting to retain possession of the ball take over as goalkeepers, so attacking moves are played in a 4-against-2 situation. However, the two goalkeepers are allowed to take part in their team's attempts to retain possession of the ball.
■ Harder:
The two goalkeepers may take part in the passing moves of the team trying to retain possession of the ball.
■ Harder:
The players on the team with possession may only touch the ball three times.

Variant 4:
One of the two goals is replaced by a target line about 15 metres long. Attackers can now collect points either by going round the goalkeeper or by dribbling the ball across the opposite target line.

Variant 5:
Timed game: the coach times how long the attackers take to score three (or five) goals. The teams then switch round. The winners are the team which succeeds in scoring the required number of goals in the shortest time.

Variant 6:
Two or three small makeshift goals (cones) are set up randomly on the pitch. The defending team (which is trying to retain possession) can score a goal by dribbling the ball through one of the small goals as part of a passing move while retaining possession of the ball.

SHOOTING AT GOAL

During their training, players must be familiarized with the situations that can arise close to goal if they are to be able to choose the cleverest, most successful option in a real match situation. Coaches must therefore regularly organize games and exercises that make new demands on the goalscoring abilities of their youngsters.

HOW THE GAME WORKS

4-a-side with dribbling across lines and shooting

A zone about 20 metres deep is marked out in the centre of the pitch between two goals (guarded by goalkeepers) approximately 50 metres apart.

Two teams play 4-a-side between the lines marking the long sides of this zone. The idea is for the players on a team to set up a passing move and dribble the ball across their opponents' line (the broken line in the diagram). The player breaking through may then take a free shoot at goal. His team retains possession of the ball whether he scores or not. However, the teams immediately change ends within the centre zone, with the goalkeeper passing to the goal scorer, who then starts off an attack aimed at the far end of the centre zone.

Duration of the game: 5 minutes

Variant 1:
After dribbling across the line marking the end of the centre zone, the attacker must dribble the ball past the goalkeeper before scoring. If the attacker is forced back during his goalscoring attempt, this is deemed null and void and the game is restarted.

Variant 2:
The teams play 3-a-side in the centre zone.
The fourth player in team A stands next to goal number one, the fourth player from team B next to goal number two.
When team A has completed its attack on goal number one, the attacker concerned trades places with his team-mate waiting next to goal number one. The substitute then initiates an attack across the far line of the centre zone. However, when team A scores in goal number two, the attacker receives a ball passed by the opposing substitute and launches an attack in the other direction.
The same procedure applies to team B.

CORRECTIVE HELP

▶ "Prepare your breakthroughs by stringing together a series of accurate passes and spreading your play."
▶ "Seize on any promising opportunity to make a determined solo run on goal."
▶ "When you have dribbled the ball and are preparing to shoot, push the ball slightly to one side."
▶ "When using your instep to shoot, keep your ankle rigid and your toes pointing downwards."
▶ "Look up again before shooting. Check where you and the goalkeeper are in relation to the goal."
▶ "When you have broken through, use an effective feint to send the goalkeeper the wrong way."

ORGANIZATIONAL TIPS

■ As many spare balls as possible must be kept ready beside both goals to avoid unnecessary stoppages.
■ The playing and recovery phases should be timed so that all the action on the ball can take place at full pace. During the breaks, coaches should give the players tips and feedback on how the exercise is progressing.
■ This exercise requires half a pitch, so a full standard pitch is required if the other players are to be occupied at the same time.

INCREASE/DECREASE THE DIFFICULTY

■ **Easier:**
Enlarging the centre zone makes it easier for the attacking team to string together a safe passing move when preparing to break through.

■ **Easier:**
The coach (or another player) can join in, serving as an extra player for the team in possession of the ball in the centre zone (five-against-four, defense outnumbered).

■ **Harder:**
The coach (or an extra player) stands in front of a goal as a (virtually passive) defender. After crossing the line, the attacker must first beat this player before being allowed to take a shot at goal.

■ **Harder:**
Once the line at the back of the centre zone has been crossed, the attacker is allowed a maximum of one (or two) touches of the ball before shooting.

Variant 3:
Here, two goals about 3 metres wide are set up on each of the lines at the back of the centre zone.
The attackers must dribble through one of the opposing team's two goals before being allowed to shoot.

Variant 4:
Here, the teams may attack across both lines and shoot at both goals. When a goal has been scored, the attacker runs back into the centre zone and his team is then given possession to mount another breakthrough attempt.

Variant 5:
Various instructions for scoring goals: Shots at goal 1 must be taken immediately after dribbling the ball across the line at the edge of the centre zone. Where goal 2 is concerned, attackers can go it alone but must take on the goalkeeper.
The two goalkeepers should occasionally change positions.

Variants:

- 4-a-side instead of 3-a-side.
- The passer plays at the back of the pitch.
- One passer is positioned on either side of the pitch.
- Following a pass into the penalty area, no more than one or two touches of the ball are allowed before shooting.

HOW THE TRAINING GAME WORKS

3-a-side with one "passer" into one goal

Marked out in front of the penalty area is a pitch measuring about 35 x 25 metres on which two teams play 3-a-side. An additional player supports the attacking team from one of the touchlines (off the pitch) by acting as a passer.
The attackers try to play their way into the penalty area. If they succeed, they may try to score a goal (without the defenders interfering). On winning the ball, the opposing team may go on the offensive after playing one pass to the passer.

Variants:

- Goals scored following a first-time sideways or pulled-back pass count double.
- An extra "neutral player" helps the attacking team build up its move.

HOW THE TRAINING GAME WORKS

3-a-side into one goal guarded by a goalkeeper

Two groups play 3-a-side into one goal guarded by a neutral goalkeeper.
After taking a shot at goal – whether successful or not – the same team retains possession and launches another attack. This is done by having the goalkeeper throw the ball out to the attacker furthest from the goal.
The teams trade places when the defending team wins the ball and passes to a team-mate outside the penalty area.

HOW THE TRAINING GAME WORKS

2-against-2 + 2 passers into two goals

Two teams of two play against each other into two goals guarded by goalkeepers on a pitch twice the size of a penalty area. The two players belonging to a third group stand on the touchlines and act as passers for the attacking team. Every two minutes, one pair on the pitch trades places with the passers.
The teams compete to see which can score the most goals.

SHOOTING # 7

Variants:

- First-time goals scored after latching on to a pass played by a passer count double.
- The passers must play first-time passes (or no more than two touches of the ball).
- Each team may involve only one of the two passers in their move.
- The size of the pitch is halved, making it the same size as a penalty area.

HOW THE TRAINING GAME WORKS

Shooting at goal against a line of four defenders

The pitch is the same size as for game 7 above, with the edge of the penalty area forming the centre-line. Two teams of four each move around their half of the pitch. One team begins a passing move within its own half, seeking to take a shot at their opponents' goal at the right moment. The opposing team tries to close down the routes to goal within its own half and block any shots.

SHOOTING # 8

Variants:

- The two teams switch round after 10 attempted shots at goal.
  The winners are the team that has scored the most goals at the end of the exercise.
- Only first-time passes (or involving no more than two touches) are allowed.
- The pass laid on for a shot at goal can also be played into the opponent's half. However, the player picking up the pass then has to shoot first-time.

HEADING # 1

Variants:

- On the way to the opposing team's goal, the ball can be caught once by a player during the heading combination and thrown to a team-mate to continue the heading move.
- Goal circles are marked out in front of both goals. Headers at goal must come from outside these circles.
- The members of the defending team cannot use their hands to keep the ball out of the goal or may only use their heads to do so.

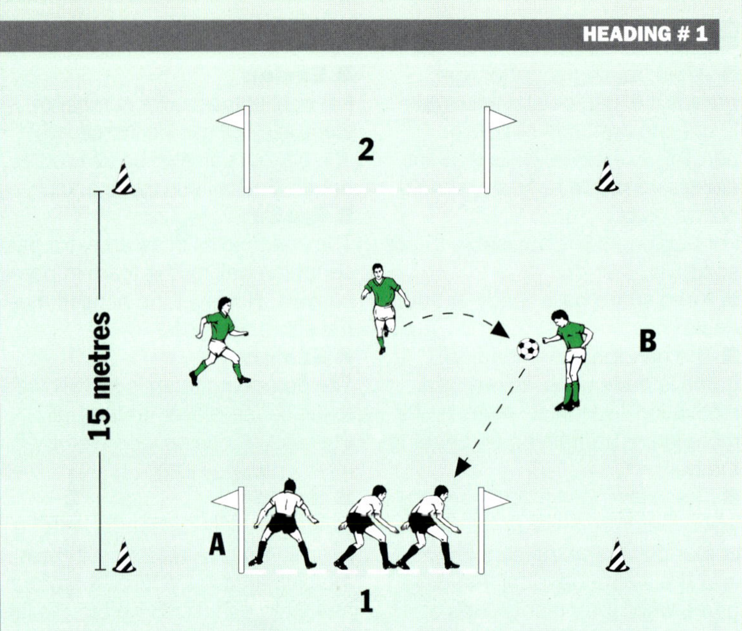

HOW THE TRAINING GAME WORKS

Heading combinations from goal to goal

Two teams of three play between two standard or makeshift goals (- marked by poles) about 15 metres apart. All the players in group A start off standing on goal line number one as goalkeepers. Team B moves forward from goal line number two, passing the ball only with their heads until they are in front of the other goal. They then try to head the ball into their opponents' goal. The teams switch round after a goal has been scored or immediately when the ball touches the ground, with the group that has lost possession running back into its own goal.

HEADING # 2

Variants:

- The ball must be headed from a standing position.
- The ball must be headed on the run, jumping off one foot.
- With points: the goal-scorer is awarded 1 point for heading a goal. The winner is the player/ team with the most points after 10 minutes.

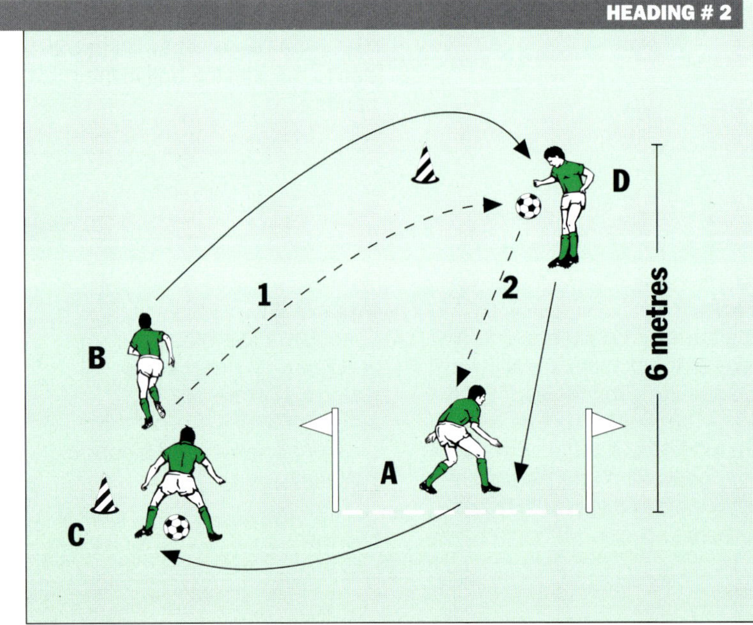

HOW THE TRAINING GAME WORKS

Headers at goal in rotation

A group of four players lines up in front of a goal as follows:
A is the goalkeeper, B and C stand next to the goal with one ball each, and D stands about 6 metres in front of the goal as the striker heading the ball.
B throws the ball to D, who heads the ball towards the goal. The players then switch positions in clockwise rotation, i.e. D becomes the goalkeeper, B the striker, goalkeeper A joins the "throwers", and C now throws the ball to B for the next attempted header on goal.

CORRECTIVE HELP

▶ "If you are a defender, always move around between your opposite number and the goal/line number one if you can."
▶ "Never try to challenge head-on an attacker from the opposing team who has the ball. Block his direct route to goal, accelerate to match his pace and then back off more slowly."
▶ "Force the attacker to try and break through on the outside, then chase him away from the goal to stop him getting into a shooting position."
▶ "Wait for the right moment to go for the ball. For example, immediately tackle any attacker who plays the ball too far away from himself."
▶ "Tackle firmly when you are running in the same direction as the attacker and can see that he will be unable to play the ball at a particular moment."
▶ "Keep your eyes on the ball only. Don't react to the attacker's body feints."

ORGANIZATIONAL TIPS

■ Enough spare balls must be kept ready by line number two to enable the new attacking move to be built up as soon as the goal-scorer has run back onto the pitch.
■ The sudden switching of the direction of play following a counter means that this game makes substantial physical and mental demands on the young players. Coaches should therefore shorten the game if they can see that the players are getting too tired.
■ Since the game focuses on teaching players how to tackle, the corrective tips and demonstrations given must concentrate on defensive play, although the game also provides practice in key elements of attacking play.

INCREASE/DECREASE THE DIFFICULTY

■ **Easier:**
Making the pitch smaller reduces the amount of space available to the players, thus making it easier for the defenders to disrupt attacking moves successfully.

■ **Easier:**
The job of the defending team will be easier if the attackers are only allowed to enter the penalty area after playing the ball through one of three goals 2 metres wide set up on the edge of the penalty area.

■ **Harder:**
Defensive play is made harder when an additional passer supports the attackers from behind. The attackers can pass back to this passer to retain possession of the ball where there is no promising opening for a breakthrough.

■ **Harder:**
The additional passers helping the attackers are not just confined to playing at the back, but may also move up and down the touchlines of the pitch.

Variant 4:
4-a-side with nominated markers following up (as in variant 2) as follows:
No goal but with a target line about 10 metres long marked out on the goal line. After breaking through into the penalty area, the attacker has to play the ball across this line in a 1-on-1 situation.

Variant 5:
The pitch for the 4-a-side game is marked out about 30 metres in front of the goal with goalkeeper. Another player acts as a "sweeper" in front of the goal. After dribbling the ball across line number one, the attackers must first also get past the "sweeper" in a 1-on-1 situation before shooting.

Variant 6:
If no goalkeeper is available, the following shooting options are possible:
– Target practice shooting at a small goal positioned on the goal line from a distance of at least 11 metres.
– The ball has to be lofted over the goal line from the edge of the penalty area.

German-language Bibliography

BAUER, G./UEBERLE, H.: Fußball, Faktoren der Leistung, Spieler- und Mannschaftsführung (Soccer, Performance Factors, Elements of Player and Team Management). Munich 1984

BISANZ, G./GERISCH, G.: Fußball. Training, Technik, Taktik (Soccer. Training, Technique, Tactics). Reinbek bei Hamburg 1995

BRÜGGEMANN, D./ALBRECHT, D.: Modernes Fußballtraining. Das systematische Lehrbuch führ Trainer, Übungsleiter, Sportlehrer, Sportstudenten und Spieler (Modern Soccer Training. The Systematic Textbook for Trainers, Coaches, Sports Teachers, Sports Students and Players). Schorndorf 1987

BRÜGGEMANN, D.: Kinder- und Jugendtraining (Children's and Junior Training). Schorndorf 1988

DEUTSCHER FUSSBALL-BUND: (German Soccer Association): Mit kleinen Spielen zum großen Spiel (From the Junior to the Senior Game). Frankfurt 1983

DEUTSCHER FUSSBALL-BUND: Mädchen spielen Fußball (Girls Playing Soccer). Frankfurt 1989

KNEBEL, K.P./HERBECK, B./HAMSEN, G.: Fußball-Funktionsgymnastik (Functional Soccer Gymnastics). Reinbek bei Hamburg 1988

KONOPKA, P.: Sporternährung. Leistungsförderung durch vollwertige und bedarfsangepaßte Ernährung (Sport Nutrition. Improving Performance Through Wholefood Nutrition Adapted to Individual Requirements). Munich 1994

DIETRICH, K.: Fußball, spielgemäß lernen, spielgemäß üben (Soccer, Learning by Playing, Practising by Playing). Schorndorf 1973

HEDDERGOTT, K.-H.: Neue Fußball-Lehre (New Textbook for Teaching Soccer). Frankfurt/M. 1973

Articles from the German Magazine for Coaches (edited by the German Soccer Federation) "fußball-training" (published by Philippka-Verlag, P.O. Box 6540, D-48034 Münster)

BOMERS, H.: Jugendfußball heute (Youth Soccer Today) (8+9/1988)

BAUER, G.: Die aktuelle Situation des Jugendtrainings (The Current Situation in Youth Training) (8+9/1988)

RECKWALD, F./CLEMENS, U.: Ohne Straßenfußball keine Talente mehr? (No More Street Soccer, No More Gifted Players?) (10/1989)

DIETRICH, K.: Kinder- und Jugendfußball im Verein (Children's and Youth Soccer at Club Level) (10/1989)

GERISCH, G./BEYER, W.: Jugendfußball – Trendwende und Perspektiven (Youth Soccer – New Trends and Future Prospects) (12/1990)

LOY, R.: Zukunftssicherung durch eine Jugendreform? (Safeguarding the Future Through Reforms at Junior Level?) (9/1991)

JERAT, W.: Wo sind die Supertechniker geblieben? (Whatever Happened to the Super Technicians?) (4/1992)

SCHMIDT, W.: Kinder werden trainiert, bevor sie selbst spielen können (Children Are Being Trained Before They Can Even Play) (5+6/1994)

HAPP, E.: Möglichkeiten und Grenzen des Kinderfußballs (Possibilities and Limitations of Children's Soccer) (5+6/1994)

PETER, R.: So kann die Schnelligkeit spielerisch verbessert werden! (Improving Speed through Play) (3/1995)

BRÜGGEMANN, D.: Talent-Förderung oder Talent-Nutzung (Promoting or Exploiting Talent?) (4/1995)

RUTEMÖLLER, E.: Den Fußball der Zukunft mit Weitsicht vorbereiten! (Soccer of the Future Must Be Prepared in a Far-Sighted Manner) (5+6/1995)

SCHOMANN, P.: Spielerisches Torschußtraining (A Playful Way to Practise Shooting) (8/1995)

Guidelines for children's soccer

Learning soccer the fun way

All kinds of mini soccer games that feature shooting at goal are the most important component of soccer training for kids. However, at the same time the 'context of play', especially the coach and parents, must offer the kids a "free playing environment" as far as possible (i.e. in particular little influence on the part of the coach, no parents telling the kids what to do).

Focus on the football

■ In principle almost all (with the exception of some tag and running games) sections of training must involve a ball. Because as an instrument of play the ball presents kids with a unique challenge.

■ Furthermore, only in this way can kids be encouraged to become increasingly skilful in controlling the ball.

Everyone can join in

■ Kids' natural energy and love of movement demands constant "activity", otherwise both the fun element and their enthusiasm soon fade. What is more, optimal learning can only be achieved if they move around and are involved in the game as much as possible.

■ Coaches of youth players must constantly remind themselves of this point when planning and organizing their training sessions.

Especially when, as is so often the case, the level of performance varies so much within one and the same group of beginners, when the teams must be skilfully put together or additional rules must be introduced to steer play in the desired direction.

Motivating training tasks

"The ball is always involved" – hopefully all youth coaches follow this rule of thumb. However, this is not enough. Forms of training involving the ball can soon become boring and monotonous if they are not "packaged" in interesting tasks of the kind that children enjoy performing. In this respect, mini forms of competition are mostly excellent at motivating kids.

Enthusiastic coach

■ If coaches want to convey a positive attitude towards soccer, then they must let their own sportiness set an example.

■ Apart from training that kids find appealing and enjoyable, the best form of motivation for children is by setting a positive example. This means that youth coaches must let their own enthusiasm for soccer shine through continually.

The individual components

Playing soccer in small groups

■ Children love to chase a ball around to their heart's content, free of all constraints.

IMPORTANT INFORMATION FOR COACHES WHO WORK WITH BEGINNERS IN SOCCER

As a result, training tasks which destroy their motivation or – worst of all – stupid forms of exercise have no place in soccer for kids! Instead, kids first have to experience and learn to love soccer as a freely played game. This lays the foundations for a lifelong enjoyment of the game.

■ As a result, the frequent mini matches, played without any constraints, must form the centrepiece of any soccer training designed for kids.

Improving individuals' technique in a fun way

■ In addition, the original game of soccer, shooting into goals, can be supplemented by interesting tasks which specifically teach kids individual aspects of football technique in a manner they will enjoy.

But up to level D youth soccer these fun tasks designed to teach kids elementary aspects of basic technique should not try to perfect their coordination or agility!

The kids should first of all only be roughly acquainted with the basic skills of the game and learn to deal with the ball in their own particular way!

Ball skills and agility

This building block constitutes the "warm-up phase" of a soccer training session designed for kids. Not only should it include interesting additional tasks that are designed to promote agility in ball handling, but it should also involve appealing games involving running (running in its various forms is the absolutely fundamental skill in soccer). Ball skills and agility constitute the basis for optimal soccer.

The aim of playing: 4-a-side/ 7-a-side

■ But training that is designed for kids or youngsters of a certain age is "only" one element. A watertight training concept must also include competitive games that promote their development.

Playing 7-a-side on a pitch measuring 36 by 55 metres is the mandatory framework for all F and E junior teams. What is more, in these lower age groups, regular 4-a-side tournaments must complement the official season of competitive games!

The *Success in soccer* videos provide all these important information for coaches who work with beginners in football.

At the same time the following guidelines determine the work involving the training and supervision of the youngest players:

- learning football the fun way
- focus on the football
- everyone can join in
- motivating training tasks
- enthusiastic coach.

The appealing, practical and age-adjusted forms of training for the youngest players are broken down into four building blocks:

- playing soccer in small groups
- improving individuals' technique in a fun way
- ball skills and agility
- the aim of playing 4-a-side/7-a-side.

On the basis of three models, coaches are shown how complete training sessions can be put together:

- training units exclusively comprising mini soccer matches
- training units as a transition between practising and playing matches
- training units as circuit training.

You can receive more information about SUCCESS IN SOCCER through Manni Klar, P.O. Box 92046, Albuquerque NM 87199, Phone: 888-828-4263; Fax: 505-232-3162, email: sifussball@aol.com (for North and South America) or Philippka-Verlag, P.O. Box 6540, D-48034 Münster, Phone +49-251-230050, Fax +49-251-2300599; email: philippka-sportverlag@T-online.de (other continents).